# Children as Philosophers

There is a growing interest in philosophy with children, based on the belief that philosophy not only enhances children's speaking, listening, reading and thinking but also promotes independence of mind and spirit, benefiting the children, their teachers and the school as a whole.

This accessible book balances an exploration of the theoretical and critical considerations of using philosophy in the classroom with real examples of children working as philosophers. Based on research by the author in a primary school, and full of practical suggestions for teachers, it demonstrates that, from a young age, children are capable of engaging in a sophisticated process of dialogue and enquiry and argues that they should have space and time to do so.

This book is the ideal starting point for teachers interested in bringing philosophy into their classroom. It is full of useful ideas for sparking off philosophical discussions, and includes helpful resources and contacts.

**Joanna Haynes** is a Senior Lecturer in Education Studies at the College of St. Mark and St. John, Plymouth.

# Children as Philosophers

Learning through enquiry
and dialogue in the primary
classroom

**Joanna Haynes**

London and New York

First published 2002
by RoutledgeFalmer
11 New Fetter Lane, London EC4P 4EE

Simultaneously published in the USA and Canada
by RoutledgeFalmer
29 West 35th Street, New York, NY 10001

*RoutledgeFalmer is an imprint of the Taylor & Francis Group*

Typeset in Sabon by
Keystroke, Jacaranda Lodge, Wolverhampton
Printed and bound in Great Britain by
TJ International Ltd, Padstow, Cornwall

*British Library Cataloguing in Publication Data*
A catalogue record for this book is available
from the British Library

*Library of Congress Cataloging in Publication Data*

Haynes, Joanna, 1953–
    Children as philosophers : learning through enquiry and dialogue
in the primary classroom / Joanna Haynes.
        p. cm.
    Includes bibliographical references and index.
    ISBN 0–415–27246–7 — ISBN 0–7507–0946–4 (pbk.)
    1. Thought and thinking—Study and teaching (Elementary)
    2. Philosophy—Study and teaching (Elementary)   3. Questioning.
    4. Discussion.  I. Title.

LB1590.3 .H394 2001
372′.0.1′9—dc21                                      2001041862

ISBN 0–750–70946–4

To the children of Lamerton C. of E. Primary School,
their families and their teachers, Jenny Thomas and
Linda Pearce.

# Contents

# List of illustrations

*Boxes*

*Figures*

# Acknowledgements

I would like to thank all those who belong to the Lamerton Primary School community, especially the children who have taken part in philosophical discussions in school and in the after-school club. I would like to thank the parents of the children and the staff at the school, who have supported and encouraged me in this work. My thanks also go to the governors of the school, for giving me permission to work with the children and to document my teaching.

I would like to thank Karin Murris for getting me started using picture books for thinking with children and for our teaching and writing partnership and friendship.

Thanks to Roger Sutcliffe and Steve Williams of Dialogueworks. I have learned a great deal from colleagues and friends in SAPERE in seminars and conferences about philosophical enquiry with children and in many conversations in the interludes.

I have benefited from discussion with colleagues and students in the primary education department at the College of St Mark and St John in Plymouth. I am very grateful to Wendy Clements for all her hard work and good humour in transcribing children's audio-recorded discussions and for her obvious enthusiasm about their content. Thanks to former colleagues who have remained friends, Fran Castle and Enid Western, for reading and commenting encouragingly on sections of the book.

Very special thanks to my son Louis for all his ideas on philosophy, and to my now grown-up daughter Georgia, who as a small girl first aroused my interest in young children's questions. Thanks to Jonny for everything. Thanks to my parents, Muriel and Bill Haynes, and to my wider family, particularly Uncle Harry, for regular expressions of interest in my writing.

Very special thanks to my friend and colleague Tony Brown, who suggested that a book should be written, got me started, told me to get on with it, listened to ideas, helped me plan and organise the material, offered constructive comments and suggestions on the writing as it appeared and applied his considerable skills as a writer and an editor to the finished draft.

Some of the material in this book has previously appeared in articles in *If . . . then* (Journal of SAPERE), in *Teaching Thinking* (Questions Publishers) and in Storywise.

J.H.
Lamerton, Devon

# Introduction

In some circles, encouraging critical thinking has for years been synonymous with good teaching. On the whole, it is associated with education at university level and sometimes with secondary pupils pursuing academic subjects at advanced level. Over the last twenty years, the idea of teaching thinking seems to have gained momentum and there are many programmes and approaches that aim to identify, practise and improve key thinking skills. University centres of research and publications in the teaching of thinking abound. Having been the province of a comparatively small number of keen and interested researchers and educators, thinking skills are now beginning to make an appearance in official curricula of schools in countries all over the world, for pupils of all ages.

As one such educator I greet the inclusion of thinking skills in the formal curriculum of schools with a mixture of enthusiasm and scepticism. As an A level student I was lucky enough to be taught by a superb teacher, who loved and knew his subject, encouraged us all to think for ourselves, to express an opinion, to argue and debate with one another, to challenge him and to be searching readers and writers. Above all he made room for us, listened and treated our ideas with an instructive balance of seriousness and humour. This experience had a profound and lasting influence on me. It is not surprising that as a teacher I should be interested in ways of deepening the thinking of students.

So why the scepticism about the teaching of thinking? I have difficulty with the view of thinking skills as a toolkit that can be built and transferred to a variety of contexts. Seen as such, there is the risk that these 'skills' will be taught in ways that fail to provoke independence of mind and spirit and fail to engender values for social, economic or environmental survival.

There is the obvious but important fact that pupils up to the legal school leaving age do not have the choice about whether to be at school or not. In Britain, the period of required attendance at school or participation in training seems to continue to grow longer. The balance between equality through universal compulsory education and freedom of the individual is highlighted in the various articles of the Convention on the Rights of the Child adopted by the UN General Assembly on 20 November 1989. Articles 12 and 13 relate to the child's right to a certain freedom of expression and Article 14 refers to freedom of thought, conscience and religion. Other articles deal with matters of discrimination, privacy, access to information and freedom of association. Article 28 calls for, as a minimum entitlement, free compulsory primary education for all. But there can be real obstacles to freedom of thought and expression in the context of compulsory schooling.

The cultivation of reasonableness through education is a means of achieving social consent about the basic principles of democracy. Democracy holds that everyone has a right to education. However, this individual right confers authority on the state to intervene in the lives of individuals by providing compulsory schooling, and on the teacher whose role it is to educate. This authority may be overt (as in traditional forms of education) or covert (as in some progressive forms of education), or it may take the form of the teacher seeking to empower the student through open deconstruction of the educational process itself (sometimes called transformative pedagogy).

For reasons of both protection and control, pupils do not enjoy equal rights or responsibilities with teachers. The right to disagree is fundamental to the idea of critical thinking and goes hand in hand with the freedom and autonomy of the individual. Critical thinking in schools is limited by the boundaries of a system where teachers not only teach but also control the behaviour of pupils through regimes of discipline and punishment. This in itself does not mean that critical thinking cannot be encouraged. It may well result in some worthwhile and instructive disturbance at those boundaries.

When it comes to matters of intellectual freedom and moral judgement there is also the political position of the teacher to consider. The public are often suspicious of the authority of the teacher. As a public servant the teacher is also under supervision by the state (Rosenow, 1993). The teacher is caught between the, often contradictory, expectations of the public and the demands of the political establishment. Teaching is more highly regulated and supervised than ever through the detail of the official curriculum and its assessment and through the system of school inspection. No stone is left unturned.

Individual teachers live and carry out their teaching work within these regulations. They go into classrooms daily and, one way or

another, they mediate the demands of the outside world in their interactions with students. They may be only too aware of the contradictions
and limitations. When it comes to the teaching of thinking and citizenship these contradictions may be at their most exposed. The challenge,
of course, is to work with the complexity and ambiguity of these
conditions, to push at the boundaries.

The episodes reported in this book are drawn from both classroom
and after-school club settings, where children have been taking part in
enquiry. Sometimes they are prompted by stories and other resources
brought by the adult or teacher. Sometimes they stem from children's
experiences.

This book is intended as a contribution to discussion about teaching
thinking in schools. It is not intended as a recipe or prescription. It
provides many examples of children working as philosophers in the
classroom. The episodes reported challenge some assumptions about
the adult's role and the authority of children.

The book is divided into four parts. The first introduces a flavour of
children's classroom discussion and suggests that our expectations
of children's thinking and provision for children's participation rights
need to be reviewed in schools. Part II explains the process of philosophical enquiry with children and discusses the relationship between
teaching thinking and teaching values. The third section explores the
kinds of demands made on teachers and learners when they get involved
in classroom enquiry. The final part explains how philosophy with
children can enhance the whole curriculum and suggests what the
benefits of philosophical enquiry in classrooms may be for both teachers
and pupils.

# Part I

# Voices from the classroom

Chapter 1 is made up of episodes of classroom conversation between the author and some primary school children. It offers interpretations of the possibilities for teaching and learning through dialogue that they contain. It briefly explains the differences between circle time and philosophical enquiry as distinctive approaches to classroom discussion.

- What's important in classroom conversation?
- How are children's ideas received?

Chapter 2 begins with the principle of children's right to participation as citizens and reports on some primary pupils' advice to teachers who may be thinking about introducing philosophy in the classroom.

- What do we understand by the right to participate as a citizen?
- What aspects of classroom life require attention if this right is to be enjoyed by children?

# 1 Thought-provoking conversations

## About death and loss

Children often talk about their experience in an honest and striking way. They seek to make their personal knowledge pertinent to the matter in hand. This is especially noticeable when exploring something like death. In the example that follows, children in a primary class were responding to a story about a widow and her pet dog, *John Brown, Rose and the Midnight Cat* (Wagner, 1977). Everything appears cosy and secure until a black cat takes to visiting the house where the widow, Rose, lives with her dog. It is a story that deals with loss and change, with jealousy and possessiveness.

In discussion, one of the children suggested that perhaps the woman's dog had taken the place of her dead husband and that the husband's spirit had somehow entered the dog. The group was taken with the notion of the husband being inside the dog, and a lively discussion followed. Stephen stopped everyone in their tracks when he spoke. Although one of the youngest in the class of juniors, his voice was clear and confident and his presence commanding. He told us that when his dad had died a few years before, his dad's spirit had entered into him. As he spoke, he touched his chest with both hands as if indicating his heart. He said, 'I've got my dad's eyes, too. And I can hear my dad talking to me and telling me what to do.'

The rest of the class seemed slightly in awe, both mystified and thoughtful. Perhaps it was shocking to think of what it might be like to have a parent die. In the classroom setting adults are often uncertain about the protocol to adopt in responding to such disclosures from children. How did what Stephen had said compare with our experience when the death of somebody very close occurred? Was Stephen's disclosure an opening for us to talk more frankly about our own perceptions of death and the spirit? We were certainly very curious and eager to ask Stephen questions. He had enabled us to move on from responding to a story to a much broader enquiry about what happens when we die. Stephen was a fairly recent arrival in the class and sometimes appeared an 'outsider'. His behaviour sometimes appeared a little odd. It could seem as if his mind was elsewhere even though he was physically present. During the minutes following his contribution about his father's death, he became something of an authority. Nobody else had the personal knowledge that allowed them to speak with such power.

## About resolving conflicts

One day, before the lesson had begun, one of the girls in a class of juniors approached me with a question. What should you do when you have had an argument and a falling-out with a friend? Something had happened in the playground and she was no longer certain whether the girl she had regarded as her best friend was still her best friend. Things had become rather heated in the dispute. The girl who reported this to me clearly felt confused and betrayed. If I had replied immediately I would probably have suggested talking about it, and as soon as possible, apologising to each other and making it up. Isn't that what adults usually advise children within the school setting? Aren't the conflicts that children experience easily resolved? Had I ever seriously considered any other options?

Instead of giving an immediate response, and reassuring her that 'everything will be all right', I decided to suggest that we put the question to the class and invite other children's responses. When we did this, one person said, 'You must say sorry straight away.' Two others suggested going away and cooling off.

I was pleased to discover that there was some divergence of experience and opinion in the group. 'Punch them on the nose!' was one boy's solution. He told us that where his family had lived before moving, their house had been repeatedly trashed. Windows were smashed and their car was damaged. He added, 'My mum says if you punch someone really hard, they don't come back.' Linda, one of the other children, commented that the trouble with that was that you might kill them without meaning to. On some occasions the boy's comment might have prompted giggles. This time, his argument was taken seriously and the truthfulness of his story acknowledged. It is an example that reminds us that we can imagine we know the circumstances of children's day-to-day lives beyond school. In fact often we know nothing of the detail and little of the general circumstances. When children introduce their personal world into discussion they highlight the different and often contradictory cultures and values that exist. As they move between home and school they may experience conflicting values on a daily basis.

I remember being struck by the realisation that, in the circumstances he described, defence of a physical kind might well be the only way to change the situation. What is the right course of action when some human beings face repeated victimisation by others? Is it wrong to retaliate when being attacked becomes intolerable? Did this boy's parents decide to take direct physical action to protect their children? Linda's explicit counter-argument made us more aware of the moral gravity and complexity of this family's position.

## About making progress and choosing suitable topics for class discussion

When discussion takes place regularly in a class, children sometimes seek a private consultation with the teacher about something that concerns them and that they think may be important for everyone. They may be looking for reassurance or permission to raise a topic, but not only that. They can be cautious, sensitive or eager about discussion of significant matters, just like any group of people. Here is a fragment of conversation with Karen, a nine-year-old girl in the class.

KAREN: Can I talk to you privately?

TEACHER: Okay. What is it?

KAREN: I don't think it's a good idea if we put our hands up and wait. Can't we just speak? Because I've forgotten what I want to say when it gets to me?.

TEACHER: It is a problem. But then some people might never get a turn. We need to try different things.

KAREN: Can I ask you something else?

TEACHER: Try me.

KAREN: Can we talk about God again in philosophy? Do you believe in God?

TEACHER: I'm not sure. What about you?

KAREN: Me too. It's easy to imagine God and Jesus when I hear stories. But some people are really convincing when they argue against it.

Both of these are on-going concerns for Karen and the group. Her private approach shows both consideration for the adult in charge and a desire to rehearse her thoughts, perhaps before she can bring them up in the larger group. What opportunities are there for children to make suggestions about ways of organising things or ways of working in the classroom? How often do teachers invite a class to offer their own questions or to revisit and review topics that have been particularly significant? Is it always necessary for the adult or teacher to determine what the starting point for questions is going to be?

As children gain in confidence they move from formulating questions of their own that are put singly to the adult. Increasingly they value the opportunity to discuss important things together as a group. They become increasingly concerned to raise questions that arise from their own lives. The following episode, like Karen's question, occurred just as the class was about to begin a session of philosophical enquiry. Susan said she knew what she really wanted to talk about because it was the thing that was most on her mind, but she thought it might upset people. It concerned a recent episode when children had witnessed an adult coming into the classroom in a state of extreme distress and anger. There had been neither damage nor physical injury but some of those who had been present had been distressed. Others had felt threatened or, at the very least, puzzled by the intruding adult's behaviour.

Such an episode could have happened anywhere. The children would certainly have witnessed such angry behaviour directly or seen it on television. Some probably experienced intense rage, frustration or upset themselves, or did so when they were younger. There was no doubt in my mind that trying to make sense of this event would be illuminating and reassuring to the children. Many adults have a role that puts them in control of children. Children are naturally concerned when they experience wild and unpredictable behaviour by adults who are out of control. It is something we all have to deal with. What can help and what can limit children's ability to make sense of the behaviour of adults, particularly when they behave in unpredictable ways? Susan's request was not made to the group as a whole but privately to me. Susan was aware that it was a sensitive issue. The angry adult was someone they all knew and was related to some of the children in the class.

I had already worked with the group on the need for confidentiality and privacy. We had already encountered the need to find ways of discussing such questions without using examples that name or compromise people we know. I asked Susan whether she felt that we could find a way to explore her questions in a philosophical way without reference to the particular incident. She told me it was too soon after the event. The incident would quickly be recognised and children in the group might be embarrassed or compromised by this. She suggested that it would have to wait. We need to honour this level of sensitivity and wisdom in children, but not in patronising ways, nor in a mood of sloppy sentimentality.

## About fantasy

In some sessions, before beginning philosophical discussion, I invite children to take a few minutes of silent relaxation with eyes closed. This is especially useful if they are obviously tired or disquieted. Relaxation helps them to make the transition from other activity to sitting still and concentrating, listening and speaking. Children often want to talk about how their thoughts wander. Here is an example of such an occasion and the wandering thoughts that were described. At the end of the few minutes of relaxation, an eight-year-old asked if she could talk about her thoughts.

'I was on the settee and a handsome man came and carried me upstairs. I was lying in my bed holding my teddy and he was beside me.'

'Sounds lovely.'

'He wasn't black.'

'What do you want to say about that?'

'Because I love black men.'

The image of a young girl being carried to the bedroom by a handsome man is the stuff of fairy tales. So what is it about this brief dialogue that is worthy of note? Is it surprising to hear a small girl expressing such pleasure and delight in a reverie about a handsome man? Does the imagery echo a fantasy, or a stereotype, associated with an adult world? Does this short conversation hold the seeds of a philosophical enquiry? How else might I have responded? Where does this all belong and where could it be taken?

## Approaches to building classroom communities

### Circle time and philosophy with children

Many adults try to make sure that there is room to explore issues of interest to the children with whom they are working. To such ends the adoption of approaches such as circle time have become an important part of the timetable in many primary schools (Mosley, 2000). In circle time, the emphasis is on building effective communication and good relationships in the class and providing a forum in which problems can be tackled constructively. Children are encouraged to explore feelings, to listen to each other, to take turns in speaking, and to seek solutions. Circle time practice includes pro-social games and activities.

Rules are established and agreed by the participants. As the name of this approach suggests, during discussion and activities children sit in a circle facing each other along with the adult in charge.

The practice of philosophical enquiry in schools is a very different approach to open-ended discussion that has grown in many countries over the last thirty years. Although children also sit in a circle for philosophical enquiry and adopt rules of interaction, that is where the resemblance to circle time ends. Central to the practice of philosophy with children is that all discussion arises from children's questions, usually in response to a particular stimulus, such as a story, picture or poem. By first examining all the questions the discussion is able to gravitate towards those questions that are open-ended and have no immediate and obvious answer. The process of choosing a question and of engaging in enquiry is a democratic one in which the adult in charge strives to enable the children's discussion to follow its own course, rather than steering it towards a planned goal. Children are encouraged to think logically, critically and creatively, to reason and reflect, and to deliberate with an open-minded disposition. The teacher models the language of philosophical discourse and introduces conceptual tools to extend or to record the development of ideas. Children collaborate, not towards unanimity, but towards shedding light from many different angles on a particular question. The drive is towards truth seeking, rather than towards resolution and convergence of opinion. Disagreement and divergence are normal and expected. Answers to questions are searched for but they are seen as provisional.

Philosophy for children has clear cognitive aims. It sets out to exercise the mind through challenging and disciplined thinking and structured interaction. It also has the social aim of teaching democratic decision-making processes. Regular participation almost certainly contributes to the development of individual self-awareness and resilience.

### The adults' responsibility

Without any prompting, many children ask philosophical questions. They are able to make use of experience and imagination in deliberating the mysteries and problems that constitute human existence. They are often persistent, and it is striking how willing children are to adopt an open disposition, which involves *changing one's mind* in the light of what one has heard. Such qualities make discussion with children pleasurable, instructive and also challenging.

Adults have to consider how the structures and boundaries they provide can extend or limit children's participation in dialogue and judgements about what is true or real, what is good or bad, what is right or unjust. At the heart of progress in such dialogue are adults' responses to what children claim to know and the ways in which power and authority are deployed.

Our perceptions of the value of children's contributions to human knowledge are influenced by beliefs about childhood and by the legal, political, economic and social systems that influence practice. Our beliefs about childhood and adulthood are not universally accepted. Our values are culturally and socially based. They need to be seen as open to influence from the changing patterns of human development. Values shift according to place and time, culture, family life and patterns of employment. They change in response to peace, crisis or conflict and according to mood and an individual's state of health.

If childhood cannot be defined or preserved, perhaps our hopes are none the less wrapped up with the idea of investing in the youngest generation, in order to make up for our mistakes. Perhaps it is our hope for them to be wiser, to avoid the mistakes that we made. Is this a means of renewal? What does our treatment of children suggest?

# 2 Making room for children to participate

You can actually do philosophy about philosophy.

(Louis, ten-year-old boy)

Is there space for children to discuss their own ideas within today's schooling, with the increasingly formalised instruction that passes for education? Can teachers justify sharing the authority of knowing what should be talked about? What do children want to talk about, anyway?

Current practice in schools tends to encourage a view of childhood as limited and inadequate, even if it does so implicitly. To counter this view, this book offers ways in which adults can work to provide children with a public voice with which to speak their mind. When children are thoughtfully vocal, their thinking and talking can help to change the classroom from a place of instruction into a place where education is possible.

Article 12 of the UN Convention on the Rights of the Child says: 'the child has a right to express a view and to have that view taken into account in any decision concerning them.' Many countries have adopted this charter but it is difficult to know whether it has had any impact at all on the lives of children in those countries. Do adults consider Article 12 in their professional and personal lives with children? Indeed, are they aware that it exists? According to UNICEF, participation rights allow children to take an active role in their communities and nations. These rights encompass the freedom to express opinions, to have a say in matters affecting their lives, to join associations and to assemble peacefully. As they grow up, the Convention suggests, children should have increased opportunities to participate in the activities of their society and to enjoy appropriate levels of responsibility as they move towards adulthood. So, legally, children enjoy the right to participation as well as to protection. Many children carry significant economic or social responsibility in their daily lives. Their particular vulnerability to exploitation or abuse need not result in a sheltering that simultaneously denies them the opportunity to make informed decisions and to influence events that concern them. Education is an area that concerns them deeply.

In many so-called civilised countries the mechanisms and opportunities for children's voices to be heard remain very limited. In England, the Children Act (1989) went some way to addressing this need, but many people associate it only with strife and conflict such as divorce or other family trauma. What stands in the way of wider recognition of children's right to have their opinions counted? What assumptions, beliefs and anxieties influence communication between adults and children? A number of things may need to change if children's right to participation is to be satisfied. Almost certainly, such changes should provoke wider debate about childhood, about relationships and power, about the nature of knowledge.

Adults could wait for national change. They could also choose to become active agents of change. It is possible for all adults to initiate change, just by changing the way they respond when children express their ideas. In fact it is possible for teachers to transform their own classrooms, simply by embarking on the approaches that form the substance of this book. The first step is to create a teaching and learning space for enquiry and dialogue. Classroom enquiry has the potential to extend the depth and range of learning experience for all those involved. It is an activity that certainly provokes attention to teaching, to facilitation of discussion and to questions of power, freedom and control in relationships among adults and children. It does call for certain skills and sensitivities to be brought into play. It is both surprising and satisfying, both demanding and comforting.

## The wisdom of children's advice to adults

A group of junior-age children who have taken part in enquiry on a regular basis were asked what advice they would want to give teachers about the practice of philosophy and discussion in school. These were some of the things they felt needed to be strongly emphasised. They are modest suggestions but have considerable potential.

- *On questioning.* Teachers need to think about what kind of questions they ask and be interested in children's questions. Teachers need to ask questions that can help children to think.
- *On listening.* Give children more time to think, to explain things to the teacher and longer to say things. Always remember children's names and things about them that they have told you.

- *On choice, participation and inclusion.* Give choice. Let children choose how to start and what to start with. Include everyone. Look at everyone's work. Try and encourage quiet ones to join in. Ask them directly what they think. (This came from a boy who rarely speaks in front of the whole class.)
- *On starting points.* Include a list of all the different kinds of material and activities that are good for philosophy. Teach in different ways.
- *On trust and approachability.* If a child has something to say let them feel they can say it to the teacher and not think to themselves, 'I'd better not tell her.'
- *On support.* Help children to ignore annoying things. Be firm so children can concentrate and not get distracted. Be kind because this helps children not to be naughty.
- *On comfort, security and attention.* Let children have a bit of meditation to shut out annoying thoughts and to relax and calm down. Help them relax and make thoughts disappear. Help them to stop fiddling. Keep reminding children to be relaxed. Let sessions be fun and not drag on. Tell children to sit comfortably and talk clearly so others can hear. Watch over children and make sure they don't hurt each other.

These themes have emerged as a consequence of my particular work with children. They are crucial areas for development. Those who work for children's participation need to continue to refine them. It's worth continuing to look for ways in which to extend our flexibility and responsiveness to children. This can be done by:

- asking questions that *seek and search* rather than ones that interrogate or manipulate debate;
- staying with *ambiguity and divergence of experience and opinion* and avoiding premature agreement and resolution, if resolution is indeed always necessary;
- understanding and working with *children's questions*;
- listening for the thoughts and feelings that lie between the words, suspending one's own response and taking time to understand what is being said;
- recognising the contributions that each individual makes and associating the contribution with the speaker;
- cultivating *attention* to the unfolding dialogue and remaining aware of the global themes;
- allowing room for intuition and receptiveness to the *about-to-be-thought-and-spoken*;

- supporting individual children to help make it possible for them to take their part;
- working in diverse ways, including *linguistic, visual, imaginative,* and *meditative*;
- recognising that teaching is a human activity in which there is a need to *work honestly and explicitly at relationships and dialogue*;
- maintaining the principle of equality in the treatment of *children as authorities* with regard to their own experience and awareness;
- *working courageously*, especially when it comes to discussing complex or sensitive issues;
- working with *care and responsibility* when monitoring the boundaries of appropriateness and safety;
- using humour and a lightness of touch for re-framing thinking and for diffusion of ideas;
- being responsive to children when preparing and planning;
- employing thoughtful reflection on the particular children's natures and interests.

What happens if adults open up classrooms and other places to children, and offer them space to think and talk philosophically? This book does not advocate a *laissez-faire* approach. Adults have to work skilfully and determinedly to support children who are acquiring complex skills. Culture works to control children as well as adults and some children find it difficult to join philosophical discussion. Part III is concerned with the particular pedagogy of philosophical enquiry and discusses strategies that adults can adopt to support children.

# Part II

# Thinking about thinking

Chapter 3 explains the processes that characterise classroom communities of philosophical enquiry and reports on the kinds of themes that are likely to be discussed. It includes an example of questions and dialogue from an infant class.

- What's involved in philosophical enquiry?
- What qualities of teaching and learning can be distinguished in this approach?

Chapter 4 seeks to engage the reader with some fundamental problems regarding knowledge, thinking and the purposes of education today. It explores various accounts of what thinking is and examines the notion of thinking skills.

- Can thinking be taught?
- What does it take to be a critical thinker?
- Do teaching thinking and teaching virtue go hand in hand?

Chapter 5 begins with a look at different approaches to teaching thinking. It compares and contrasts philosophy with children with other ways of working. It traces the roots of philosophy with children and explains its broad educational aims. It suggests that the community of enquiry is a way of including children as citizens.

- How does philosophy with children compare with other ways of teaching thinking?
- What are the educational aims of philosophy with children?
- What does philosophy with children have to do with citizenship?

# 3 A distinctive approach to learning through discussion

The main activity of the community of philosophical enquiry is whole-class discussion where the classroom organisation may vary from week to week. A topic may be carried over several sittings, often enhanced by the interludes that provide time for digestion of ideas. Participants sit together in a way that enables each person to hear and see all the others. Ground rules for working together are agreed and can be modified as the group develops. These rules are explicitly addressed at the outset but are gradually internalised by the participants and thus become, according to Quinn (1997), the hallmark of real social and intellectual engagement.

Rules include all the obvious prerequisites of ordered and fair deliberation. Listen carefully, avoid interrupting or dominating, respect one another and don't ridicule. Silence is accepted although the reticent are gently encouraged. In a review, following a term's work in an infant class, one seven-year-old said, 'I've enjoyed philosophy a lot, but I'd really like to know what Kathryn thinks.'

Kathryn had barely spoken in the group, and others expressed a similar wish. These comments from her peers signalled to Kathryn that her friends were willing to listen to her, and their interest in her gave her some gentle encouragement to make her views known. In another class, this time of juniors, one girl was silent for the first six weeks, whilst it seemed that most other members of the class expressed their every thought. In the seventh session, when she did speak, it was with great coherence and clarity and the rest of the class was attentive to her every word.

In the early stages of the development of a community of enquiry the teacher usually provides a starting point for questions. Teachers can use some text to read aloud, such as a story, poem or newspaper report. They may bring an object or play a piece of music, or show a set of photographs or a documentary film. Later on, children may draw on questions from other sources that they have chosen. Or they start from questions that arise directly from their experience.

Teachers need to select materials carefully on the basis of their power to express ambiguity, to produce puzzlement, or to evoke a deep response. The illustrations in books are just as important as the text in prompting questions and establishing reference points for discussion.

Murris & Haynes (2000) provide both detailed guidance and a selection of sources in their Storywise series. There are also resources such as the novels of Matthew Lipman including *Pixie* (1981) and *Lisa* (1985) that have been designed to provide a comprehensive programme of philosophy for both younger and older pupils. Robert Fisher has produced a series of books grouping, for example, stories (1996) and games (1997) selected to promote thinking in the classroom. Another approach uses high-quality picture books, or video animation of picture book stories. Picture books are already available in classrooms, and their use for enquiry is detailed by Murris (1992). There are a number of stories and videos that are particularly suitable for very young children, including those in nursery and pre-school groups. There is a section on resources for philosophical enquiry in classrooms at the end of this book.

Once the material has been introduced and made accessible to all the pupils, the children who have participated need to take time to think. This time may be spent in silence, or in talking to a neighbour. Depending on age and mood, children can draw or write notes in response to the stimulus. Children consider their own responses and are encouraged to formulate questions. It is the examination and pursuit of the children's questions that form the substantial part of each enquiry. The teacher does not offer questions unless invited to do so by the children.

The discourse cannot and should not be separated from the behaviour of the participants. They need to be seen as one. Attention needs to be paid to the behavioural and thinking elements of careful listening or giving reasons for a particular statement. Ideas need to be explored. It may be helpful to think of it as a time when children's ideas are being handled, manipulated, moulded, shaped or unpicked. This means that a range of activities, such as drawing, painting and drama, can provide a vital part of the philosophical enterprise. Movement and change in the focus of the children's attention is not only possible, it is a natural habit. Teachers need to accept it and work with it, sometimes encouraging children to stay a little longer with a topic, sometimes moving on following the flow of the children's natural curiosity.

Classroom philosophy is a practical activity rather than a purely cerebral one. The practice of classroom philosophy is collaborative

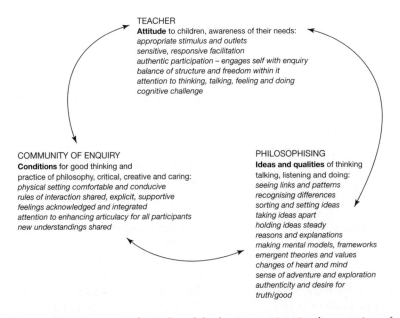

TEACHER
**Attitude** to children, awareness of their needs:
*appropriate stimulus and outlets*
*sensitive, responsive facilitation*
*authentic participation – engages self with enquiry*
*balance of structure and freedom within it*
*attention to thinking, talking, feeling and doing*
*cognitive challenge*

COMMUNITY OF ENQUIRY
**Conditions** for good thinking and
practice of philosophy, critical, creative and caring:
*physical setting comfortable and conducive*
*rules of interaction shared, explicit, supportive*
*feelings acknowledged and integrated*
*attention to enhancing articulacy for all participants*
*new understandings shared*

PHILOSOPHISING
**Ideas and qualities** of thinking
talking, listening and doing:
*seeing links and patterns*
*recognising differences*
*sorting and setting ideas*
*taking ideas apart*
*holding ideas steady*
*reasons and explanations*
*making mental models, frameworks*
*emergent theories and values*
*changes of heart and mind*
*sense of adventure and exploration*
*authenticity and desire for*
*truth/good*

*Figure 1* Involvement of mind and body: integration in the practice of philosophy

and collective as well as individual. Individual children, like adults, have strengths in different areas, such as logical reasoning, imaginative ideas, the ability to see the whole, awareness of others, the expression of empathy, the ability to spot patterns and connections, and the ability to see flaws in a line of argument. Successful engagement depends on the freedom of interaction of such divergent and complementary strengths within a group.

## What kinds of things do children discuss?

Topics are wide-ranging. Issues I have discussed with primary school children include friendship, secrets, bullying, differences, anger, punishment, life and death, personal identity, human consciousness, animal consciousness, thinking and knowing, religious beliefs, the concept of mind, the origin of language, imagination, dreaming and reality, goodness, fairness, justice and truth.

Proper time and space must be provided for children to explore their own questions and to play with ideas. The teacher's role is to prompt children into giving reasons for their ideas, making distinctions and connections, constructing arguments and developing hypotheses and analogies. A balance has to be struck between a sense of adventure and exploration and a sense of direction and progress. The teacher helps the group to clarify and build on ideas whilst allowing the discussion to follow its own course. Splitter and Sharp (1995: 169) suggest that:

> Inquiry begins with what is given, which includes children's beliefs, attitudes and unreflective opinions. In order to avoid the twin evils of manipulating the child into a predetermined moral frame, and presenting ethical enquiry as a collection of barren procedures and techniques whose outcomes are of no real significance, that which each child brings to the inquiry must be duly acknowledged and incorporated.

The enquiry process is not suited to impromptu meetings on odd occasions when there are a few spare minutes. Regular meetings are necessary. Children are then able to manage the routines and practise the necessary self-control and build up confidence in articulating their views. They will look forward to the next meeting and reflect on the discussions of the previous sessions. When the group meets on a regular basis, the questions that children ask become more thoughtful. Deeper links are made between the various subjects explored. The development of self-regulation and reasonableness rests partly upon the content of the enquiry. Of course, the quality of each meeting is partly determined by the individual and collective dispositions as well as the shared practice of increasingly sophisticated questioning and sustained discourse.

## An example of work with children aged four to seven years

This episode is interesting because of its very explicit references to moral concepts. The discussion was prompted by a story about three robbers. The story goes something like this.

The fierce robbers stole from passing carriages. People were frightened of them. They were threatening and violent. They had a cave in the mountains where they stored their treasure. One night they stopped a carriage only to find Tiffany, a little orphan girl. She was pleased to see them, as she was being taken to live with a wicked aunt. As there was no treasure, the robbers stole her. They wrapped Tiffany in a cape and took her away to their cave, where they gave her a comfortable bed to sleep in. Tiffany found their treasure and asked them what it was for. The robbers had no answer. They coughed and spluttered.

*Figure 2* John asked, 'Why did the robbers steal?'

They had never thought of spending their wealth. They then decided to use the money to buy a castle. They gathered up lost and abandoned children to live there. People began leaving poor, abandoned children at their doorstep. The children grew up, married and had children of their own. Many years later the robbers died and the children built three tall towers in their memory.

This story prompted the following questions from a class of five- to seven-year-olds.

Did the robbers change into good people?
How did all the children arrive at the door?
Why did the robbers take the children?
Why did the robbers steal/snatch the treasure?
Why did the bad robbers give all the treasure away?
Who looked after the children?
Why did people build three tall towers for the robbers?
Why were all the children dressed in red clothes?
Why were the robbers blue?
How did all the houses get built so quickly/how did the children build the houses?
How did the robbers find the castle?

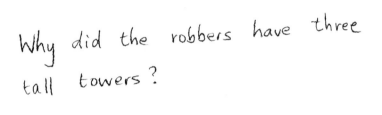

Why did the robbers have three tall towers?

Robert

*Figure 3* The teacher scribed Robert's question for him. 'Why did the robbers have three tall towers?'

In the following extract the children are discussing the first question, 'Did the robbers change into good people?' What follows are the major threads of the children's enquiry and some indication of the teacher's role in supporting the exploration of the children's ideas.

TOM:  The robbers were nice at the end because they made houses for the children.
PATSY:  Robbers don't normally pick up babies.

DAVID: The baby wasn't at the church, he was at the doorstep of the robbers' house.

TEACHER: So what do you think happened?

DAVID: I was – think, the robbers, another person took it and brought it to the doorstep.

TEACHER: Somebody brought the baby to the robbers, they didn't take it?

ANDREW: They probably started taking children because they had taken a child from the carriage.

DAVID: I think the robbers took all the children to dress up then they went in the church.

TEACHER: Why?

DAVID: Because they weren't wearing red before they went into the church.

TEACHER: But why should the robbers want to do that?

DAVID: Because the people in there have to wear red stuff when they go in there.

TOM: The baby was crying and one robber came up and the robber picked up the baby and it stopped crying.

TEACHER: What do you make of that?

TOM: I don't know how robbers can stop babies crying.

KIRSTY: 'Cos they've never had a baby, so normally they wouldn't know how to control a baby if it cries.

TEACHER: They built three tall towers in memory of their foster fathers. What does that mean?

KAREN: Is it, um, a dad but not your real dad?

DAVID: It's like a baby sitter.

TEACHER: Why did they call the three robbers their foster fathers?

KAREN: They cared for them, they gave them drinks and food.

KIRSTY: They cared for them and made houses for them to live in when they were older.

KIRSTY: They were mean robbers to start with but once they got more children they became nicer.

JAMES: If you get more children you have to be nice, then you can stop robbing. They don't want to see you nasty.

BRIGID: Because they saw how the children grew up and they knew how to grow up and they started to be nice.

DAVID: I think why did the robbers snatch the treasure?

TEACHER: Why did they start stealing?

KAREN: Because they were nasty.

KIRSTY: No, they could have just stole because they wanted to have some money to buy stuff for their houses and food and drinks.

DAVID:  They were stealing because they was nasty because there were
rings in the treasure box.

LINDA:  I think they were stealing so they could buy all the children a
great big house.

This was only the fifth occasion this group of children had met to work
together in this way. The episode demonstrates the children's ability
to address a complex moral question of their own. They were able to
identify relevant evidence and to weigh it up. The teacher's questions
re-state what a child has said, sometimes rephrasing it, for the purposes
of clarification and to encourage further thinking. The teacher also
checks that the children understand the language used in the story.
Children are clearly able to pay attention to the accuracy and detail
of events. They explore various incidents in order to make sense of
the characters and they speculate about the motives of the robbers as
well as trying to account for the changes in their behaviour. They are
able to respond to one another's ideas and to challenge each other.
The speculation (from Kirsty, James and Brigid) about the influence that
looking after children might exert on the behaviour of the robbers shows
considerable insight into the potential of caring relationships.

## Moral and pedagogical demands on the teacher

In a community of philosophical enquiry the teacher does not know
the precise content of the lesson in advance. Rather it is determined by
the children's questions. Answers are provisional, and this is somewhat
at odds with the curricula of schools in many countries, where the
emphasis is often on very precise learning objectives and outcomes. This
way of working opens up the debate about the purpose of teachers'
planning, preparation for effective teaching and what styles of teaching
are appropriate.

Teachers have to be willing to treat pupils' questions without prejudice
and to genuinely commit themselves to the enquiry. They need to resist
a natural desire to lead the discussion in a planned direction and must
avoid the temptation to show children that 'teacher knows what's best'.
The teacher's skills are crucial to the success of enquiry-based methods
of teaching. The teacher's presence, attention and responsiveness during
the enquiry are of the utmost importance in supporting the children's
experience of thinking for themselves. Bonnett (1995: 306) writes that:

> Teaching in respect of thinking will perhaps be much more a case
> of letting pupils think than instructing them – though the 'letting'

is not simply passive, but rather, itself responsive. For the teacher it is harder than for the learner, for the teacher has somehow to endeavour to be open – to think in the demanding sense – both with regard to that which calls to be thought by the content and the learner.

Bonnett argues that teaching in this way requires certain virtues in the teacher: patience and the ability to hold back, faith in the usefulness of thinking that is difficult and challenging, charity in maintaining an open disposition towards the thoughts of others.

## The process of enquiry: a summary

The following points summarise the process of this type of philosophical enquiry as a whole. It should be treated as a framework to facilitate enquiry, rather than an organisational blueprint to be followed mechanically. It may take several sessions to complete the cycle. There may be several diversions along the way. Each class adapts the process according to the direction that the enquiry takes.

- *Getting started.* Children agree rules of interaction or they are reminded of those already agreed. They may choose to work at one particular thing, such as listening carefully to each other or trying to give reasons or examples to back up their ideas. Sometimes children begin with some minutes of silence or relaxation to prepare for the work they are about to do.
- *Sharing a stimulus to prompt enquiry.* The teacher introduces a story, a poem, a picture, a piece of music, which is studied and enjoyed by the class altogether. As the class become accustomed to working in this way, pupils themselves want to suggest starting points. Children are invited to consider their response and, in particular, anything that puzzles them.
- *Pause for thought.* Everyone is invited to take some time to think about different ideas that come to mind in response to the stimulus. Sometimes children sit quietly thinking alone, sometimes they talk in pairs or small groups, exchanging ideas. Pencils and paper are made available for those who want to draw or jot down their thinking.
- *Questioning.* Questions are recorded for all to see. They may come from individuals or as a result of paired and group work. Older children can write up their own questions. The teacher is careful to record questions accurately, according to the words

used by the questioner. Anyone can ask for clarification about a question.

- *Connections.* Links are made between questions. They may be moved around and grouped. In the process of making connections, children also draw distinctions.

- *Choosing a question to begin enquiry.* There are lots of different ways of doing this and the teacher's job is to ensure that the process is inclusive and fair. Children may vote, pick a question out of a hat or start at the beginning of the list and work down. Sometimes this stage is omitted because a discussion has already begun in the process of making connections between questions.

- *Building on each other's ideas.* The teacher has to work hard to encourage listening, considered responses and deep exploration. A balance has to be struck between encouraging children to follow on from one another's ideas and allowing related lines of enquiry to open up. Sometimes there are several threads of discussion.

- *Recording discussion.* Developing the enquiry can sometimes involve a graphic mapping of ideas through a web, concept map or Venn diagram. This helps to keep track of different aspects of discussion and also means that the material can be saved for future continuation or for children to add to between sessions.

- *Closure and review.* The teacher may summarise verbally or refer to written records. Participants may be invited to have the last word. Children may be offered a follow-up activity. Resolution is rare – new questions are more common. Both teacher and pupils sometimes reflect on the process itself, or their own participation in it – How did we do? Did we listen to each other? What progress have we made? Have we changed our minds?

# 4 What kind of thinking are we teaching?

There is a deep-seated confusion in society over the purposes of education, and even those people who have thought long and carefully about its purpose often cannot agree. Coupled with this is a certain dissatisfaction felt by many people who are involved in education. The direction in which education should go is something that society finds it difficult to be confident about.

If you talk to teachers, parents and children one thing becomes clear. They all want education to be a successful experience for those who undergo it. People want education to work, and those who express the greatest satisfaction are those who not only feel a personal commitment to their own education but also feel valued by those who educate them.

Although we are not sure how it should be done, almost everyone agrees that self-respect and respect for others should be a result of having been educated. It does seem that in some ways we value knowledge more than understanding, and wisdom even less. There is plenty of advice from beyond the world of education. The nuclear physicist Sir Mark Oliphant is quoted as saying, 'Knowledge on its own is useless, unless it leads to a greater respect for others' (Jackson, 1999).

Midgley (1995: 21) writes:

> Thinking out how to live is a more basic and urgent use of the human intellect than the discovery of any fact whatsoever, and the considerations it reveals ought to guide us in our search for knowledge, as they ought in every other project we pursue.

Gardner (1999) is also vocal about the need to redefine intelligence in keeping with the times and for its association with certain virtues. In recognition of the environmental problems we need to resolve, 'species humility' is the virtue he nominates for cultivation in the twenty-first century.

But this linking of knowing and moral application, or knowing action, is not new. Nor is the idea of recognising different forms of knowing and their interdependence. Children recognise this, too, as Linda, an eleven-year-old primary school pupil, showed in another way when she said, 'You've got different kinds of knowledge. There's general knowledge and there's personal knowledge, and nobody knows everything.' Woods and Jeffrey (1996) contains a rich discussion of ways in which teachers seek to make public knowledge more relevant and accessible to children by making room for personal and for possibility knowledge.

Six hundred years before the birth of Jesus of Nazareth the Chinese sage and philosopher Lao-Tzu became the inspiration for Taoism and later the Tao-te-Ching, or Way of Power. With its teaching of self-sufficiency, simplicity, detachment and veneration of the feminine qualities, Taoism suggests that what *is* and what *is not* offer harmony through complementarity.

> Thirty spokes join at the hub;
> Their use for the cart
> Is where they are not.
> When the potter's wheel makes a pot,
> The use of the pot
> Is precisely where there is nothing.
> When you open doors and windows for a room,
> It is where there is nothing
> That they are useful to the room.
> Therefore being (what is manifest) is for benefit
> Non-being (what is hidden) is for usefulness.
>                                    (Lao Tzu, 1963)

What are the complementary elements of schooling and education, and where is the harmony? If we desire children to gain knowledge, Lao-Tzu would have us think about the way to this powerful knowledge. Perhaps we would do well to gain some degree of self-sufficiency, simplicity and, with it, some ability to detach ourselves from the cycle of studying facts and testing for memorisation.

## Letting enquiry loose in the classroom

From an early age, and provided they are not ignored, children ask questions with philosophical potential such as:

Am I real?
How do thoughts get into your mind?
Where did the first chickens come from?
How do you know when you're dreaming?
Why do people have secrets?
Why do husbands split up from their wives?

The horizons of such questions are not boundless but the mystification they express is profound. Part of the appeal of such questions is that they are not drawn from within the confines of what, through schooling, we come to know as the 'subjects' within the framework of knowledge. They take us away from these narrow paths and beyond to bigger and deeper spaces of knowing and being, where the edges are blurred or beyond our reckoning.

These children's searches can be extended and sustained. This is best done when children are given opportunities to be included in conversations that take their experience and their perceptions of the world seriously. Many adults who enjoy working with children say that what gives them the greatest pleasure in their work is children's ability to pose challenging questions and their curiosity and eagerness to learn. Most teachers want to be party to children's perceptions of the world. They want to know how younger human beings see things and they acknowledge the diversity of perspectives among them. They value their conversations with children precisely because these conversations break out of the mould of the accustomed and the known, into the realm of the mysterious and the puzzling. Teachers value the poetic, the philosophical, the lateral, original and imaginative thinking that unschooled minds bring to our often taken-for-granted and familiar world.

We can consider the concept of theory as 'a vehicle for thinking otherwise' (Ball, 1994). The challenge to *think otherwise* serves to enrich the search for knowledge and understanding. We need to make room in the classroom, for 'otherwiseness'. But such a move exists in a curious tension, since it cannot be written into the official curriculum.

While the need for teachers to secure learners' interest and motivation in the classroom is taken as self-evident, what is mentioned less often in debate about curriculum or pedagogy is provision for everybody's intellectual excitement and for teaching that departs from predictability and routine. Philosophical enquiry, in its instructive avoidance of final resolution or hard-and-fast answers, provides exceptional freedom and discipline for adults and children. There are answers, but they are only temporary.

Of course, teachers are drawn to explore philosophical enquiry in their classrooms for a variety of reasons. Among the most frequently mentioned benefits are the development of higher-order thinking skills, moral, social and personal development, and education for citizenship. These are not neutral areas of the curriculum. They are all richly controversial and problematic areas, where conflicting beliefs about knowledge, rights, responsibilities and power are rife.

## Schools of thought on thinking! Can thinking be taught?

Many people who are concerned with education have put forward the argument that young people need to be taught to think critically and logically, to analyse ideas, to organise sound arguments and to make well informed judgements. Jonathon Glover, of the University of London, writes about ethics and moral philosophy. One of his arguments is that teaching people to think rationally and critically can make a difference to their susceptibility to false ideologies (Glover, 2001). In his research into atrocities committed by ordinary human beings all over the world during the twentieth century he suggests that those communities that have succeeded in resisting dictatorship, cruelty and acts of torture are those that nurture what he calls 'the benign rebel' in their children. In the *Guardian* (13 October 1999) James Meek quotes him as saying:

> If you look at the people who sheltered Jews under the Nazis, you find a number of things about them. One is that they tended to have different kinds of upbringing from the average person, they tended to be brought up in a non-authoritarian way, brought up to have sympathy with other people and to discuss things, rather than just do what they were told.

What would an education of the benign rebel look like? The politicising of education by successive governments has left a long list of what they require of state schools. If we think about the pressure that governments have put schools under it is no wonder that they bow to both political and economic demands. Is the benign rebel (either adult or child) likely to be nurtured in today's schools?

Some people of course believe that, as technology advances, schools in their present form will disappear. If this is so, how will young people learn resilience, resistance and the will to challenge authority? Would people in Britain know how to resist a dictator? Do they know how to care for immigrants and political refugees?

Does the World Wide Web challenge the traditional authority of the teacher and of schools? Does it offer the possibility of greater individual autonomy and the creation of new knowledge networks and communities outside the authority of the state?

## The tradition of critical thinking

Teachers who encourage questioning and critical thinking in their pupils are engaging in a practice that has been fundamental to the concept of a rounded education in a democracy. Teaching pupils to think for themselves, to question received knowledge and to learn through challenge, scrutiny and deliberation of ideas has been at the very heart of a view of education that espouses creativity, invention and progress. Magee (1998: 25) writes that:

> Ancient Greece was the first society in which students were taught to think for themselves – to discuss, debate, argue and criticise – and not just to parrot the views of their teacher. It led to the most rapid expansion of understanding there had ever been and to the idea that knowledge can actually grow through criticism.

The idea of *critical* thinking and scrutiny as a philosophical method in itself needs careful examination. Critical thinking includes being able to distinguish between different ideas and to identify the assumptions, inconsistencies and weaknesses in thinking and reasoning. There is indeed a sense of progress when children demonstrate the ability to clarify an idea, as Tim does here, in a class discussion.

> I disagree with Robert because we're not saying a slug doesn't have a brain. We're saying it doesn't think. And thinking and brains are two totally different things, 'cos you cannot think and still have a brain . . . [Other children request clarification] . . . Well, if you don't have a brain you can't think but if you have a brain you don't have to think . . .
>
> (Community of enquiry, mixed junior class)

Philosophical dialogue offers good opportunities to take part in conceptual analysis, to use logical thinking and to engage with nuances of meaning and interpretation. As a result, children learn to point out inconsistencies in argument and the need to consider many examples in order to judge whether something may be true or not. They do this through direct collaborative participation in discussion of issues that they have chosen, rather than by working one by one through a taxonomy of critical thinking skills.

Children also come to recognise the ways in which language shapes our thinking. We use metaphors so routinely that we may not notice them in our speech, as Karin Murris shows us. 'On the surface, everyday language seems to clarify our thinking about issues, but it is only when examining it in more detail we realise that many "habits of thought" have their roots in everyday language' (1997: 18).

Children get most excited when meeting concepts of mind and thought. 'Can your mind be empty?' 'Can you switch your mind on and off?' 'Can thoughts get lost?' It is at this point, when they struggle to make sense of metaphors, that they can begin to complain that their brains are hurting. The effort of thinking under the metaphor and behind the words can be almost painful. This is part of the exciting struggle to think 'otherwise'.

## Changing our minds

Critical thinking skills, such as making distinctions and connections and recognising inconsistencies in an argument, are not necessarily sufficient to enable children to be critical in the full sense of the word. So what is required for a child to question or challenge the ideas of another person, particularly an adult in a position of authority? As Magee says in the quotation above, the purpose of education is 'not just to parrot the views of a teacher'. How can teachers learn to welcome such challenges in the classroom? Where do the boundaries of a teacher's responsibility and authority lie? Quinn (1997) has written about the importance of teaching children to be critical in their thinking, partly to avoid what he calls intellectual vices, and partly in order to develop their strength to resist the pressure of persuasion from more powerful or articulate others. His teaching techniques include subjecting older junior pupils to what he calls 'provocation'. In this practice Quinn acknowledges both the emotional dimensions of critical thinking and the problem of translating belief into action.

An open-minded attitude is one that never takes anything for granted and continuously questions assumptions. Philosophical puzzlement is in itself an emotional condition involving doubt and uncertainty. It may give rise to feelings of alienation, despair or excitement. In an enquiry emerging from children's ideas about human beings having spirits or souls, Graham, aged eight, expressed the most profound disquiet about whether his aunt's spirit would have had the chance to leave her body when she died in a house fire. His face showed how much this mattered to him, and it also mattered to everyone else present during the enquiry. Asking questions, and giving and taking criticism, require confidence and flexibility. In a discussion Cathy showed that she had, for the present, reached her limits of acceptable challenge when she said, 'I think we should stop talking about this now because I believe one thing and other people believe something different. We should be allowed to believe what we want to believe.'

Being the only person in a group to disagree with a particular view can feel risky. Moral issues, by their very nature, invoke our deepest passions. Offering challenges to ideas in a way that respects the other person requires an empathetic outlook.

## Ethical features of thinking

In his autobiography *Killing Time* (1994) the philosopher Paul Feyerabend concluded that a moral character could not be created by any kind of planned intervention, educational or otherwise. He regarded it as a gift dependent on:

> accidents such as parental affection, some kind of stability, friendship, and – following therefrom – on a delicate balance between self-confidence and a concern for others. We can create conditions to favor the balance; we cannot create the balance itself.
>
> (1994: 174)

Guy Claxton in his book *Wise Up* (1999) also suggests that the best thinkers are not taught but given room to think. The community of philosophical enquiry concerns itself with establishing these conditions and room for thinking. Matthew Lipman (1991) deals with these dimensions of learning in enquiry when he uses the term 'caring thinking'. He argues that education for good thinking requires caring thinking to be taught alongside critical and creative thinking, the manner of teaching being crucial. These different ways of thinking reflect the branches of philosophy called ethics, aesthetics and epistemology. They deal with ideas of goodness, beauty, knowledge and truth.

Is it possible to see evidence of caring thinking in action during a meeting of a weekly philosophy club where Karen testifies to the caring process when she refers to the opportunity to raise issues for discussion?

> Well, I think it just helps you to think that life's not just one big worry. You can talk about new things and make new friends and

you share your problems, get advice from other people on what to
do, and how you can make it better and everything.

(Philosophy Club, 1998)

Karen's comments refer directly to the use pupils made of the community of enquiry to explore a real-life problem in a philosophical way.
This group, having worked together for some time, was in the habit of
asking significant questions that arose from direct experience. They no
longer relied only on the teacher to offer the initial stimulus for questions
and discussion in the form of a story, poem, a piece of music or a picture.
Not only does the community of enquiry tackle matters that have a
bearing on how we behave as human beings towards one another, it
also plays a part in teaching us more about the nature of feeling and
emotion as dimensions of moment-by-moment thinking and action.

## Self-management and reasonableness

It is neither possible nor desirable to engage in philosophical enquiry
purely at a cognitive level. Adults and children have to get to grips
with thinking and discussion at another level. They need to develop
sensitivity, compassion and concern for the well-being of others. These
need to be balanced with an authentic search for truth and truthfulness.
As well as being able to make defensible moral judgements, children
need to be aware of their own feelings and those of others. They need
to know the part that feelings play in the acceptance or rejection of
a particular belief. This means they have to pursue the tricky business
of self-management. They need to learn what to do with feelings and
how to learn with them, or in spite of them. This can be both profoundly
satisfying and terribly difficult. It means investigating or coming to
recognise different ways of knowing and different ways of learning.

Following the democratic educational ideals of philosophers such
as John Dewey, some proponents of *Philosophy with Children*
prefer the goal of 'reasonableness' to the goal of rationality *per se*.
Reasonableness is more than rationality. Splitter and Sharp (1995) argue
that reasonableness is primarily a social disposition, involving beliefs,
attitudes and habits which bridge the gap between thought and action.
Linda, aged ten, also reports the benefit of reasonableness that philosophical enquiry can bring when she says, 'I find the rules for philosophy
useful when I go home because every time I go to shout at my brother
I just use those rules to calm down.'

In an everyday context Linda's comment reveals the interplay of
thought, feeling and action. For Linda philosophy has direct and practical

application. The rules she refers to have evolved in the community of enquiry both during classroom work and in the after-school Philosophy Club. The 'rules' she describes include techniques that the group had practised (at their own request) for calming down and avoiding distractions. Also included were edicts that they tried to stick to, such as listening to each other without interrupting. The children had explored the gap between knowing what seems right or sensible and doing what seems right or sensible.

As well as taking delight in epistemology and metaphysics, children also want to address the moral dimensions of their own lives. They see the community of philosophical enquiry as a place where this can be done. Teachers who commit themselves to philosophising with children not only seek to promote logical and critical thinking by encouraging thoroughness and rigour, they also seek to provide support so that children can be adventurous and bold. In Wittgenstein's words, 'You could attach prices to thoughts. Some cost a lot, some a little. And how does one pay for thoughts? The answer, I think, is: with courage' (quoted in Corradi Fiumara, 1992).

## Thinking skills?

Numerous attempts to identify and categorise different kinds of thinking have followed from the drive to expand and improve knowledge creation and to remove obstacles to learning. What is it that expert thinkers do? Perhaps if we knew what it is that expert thinkers do we could use the knowledge to help children further their skills. Can the essence of the experts be captured and taught?

The thinking skills thesis has certainly caught the interest of many, but popularity shouldn't, of itself, be taken as proof. Some degree of scepticism is useful, coupled with the exploration of ways to challenge the ideas promoted by the thinking skills lobby.

The enthusiasm for thinking skills as a solution to our difficulties with the curriculum stems partly from concern that what is offered in schools today fails to keep up with current ideas about effective work practice, leisure pursuits and the desire for good-quality relationships. We know that youngsters today will need a plethora of skills to survive as adults and we also know that some of those skills have yet to be invented. We are also fond of the past, and some of the traditional values of schools sound very attractive to us in our less secure moments. But is it possible to forge an education for children that will help them in the twenty-first century, using a curriculum that has many features of the nineteenth century still firmly embedded in it? If we teach thinking, it is argued, we will create a currency that can be exchanged in unimagined or unpredictable futures.

Michael Bonnett (1995) argues that the appeal of a core of transferable skills is that it trades on nuances of empowerment. But where and how is this empowerment to be achieved? It is doubtful whether many children, or their teachers, would list feeling empowered in their top ten school experiences. The question of whether the skills that are often associated with thinking exist as specific competences and abilities is questionable. The notion that they can be taught and applied to *content* reflects a fundamental view of our relationship with the world. Bonnett writes, 'Essentially, content becomes something to be scrutinised, worked upon, analysed, manipulated, given shape . . . [the thesis] expresses content as a disconnection between thinker and the world, thinker and truth' (p. 301).

Bonnett mounts a powerful attack on the thinking skills approach, which he portrays as instrumentalist in its desire to make the environment, including the world of meanings, a resource. He rejects this perspective on the relationship between thinking and content, and characterises it instead as 'an open engagement imbued with a sense of the unknown' (p. 304). In many situations it is our sense of the unknown, the hidden, that provokes us to think, that draws out our thinking and pulls us towards the not-yet-thought.

## Beyond thinking skills: philosophy as a way of life

If we are concerned to develop our thinking, we need to move beyond an overly structured, narrow and rigid tradition of logical thinking and argument. This is particularly the case when that type of thinking takes us always in the direction of closure, polarisation and the irreconcilable, and away from solution, decision or ambiguity and suspended judgement. Our habitual ways of thinking must allow us to live, in the full sense of the word, with rapid change and uncertainty, with unprecedented adjustments in time and motion as well as with the ordinariness of everyday life, with highly intelligent technology and with the enormous power of information management.

Anthony Stevens, a Jungian psychotherapist, gave a lecture at the Ways with Words festival at Dartington Hall entitled 'The Millennium Phenomenon and Apocalyptic Thinking' to mark the final months of 1999. He argued that reason is not enough to deal with many of the things we are likely to face in the future. He suggested that we require nothing short of a 'psychic earthquake'. Perhaps this in itself is an example of apocalyptic thinking. We cannot possibly know what we will need to know.

The German philosopher Martin Heidegger argued that 'we can learn thinking only if we radically unlearn what thinking has been traditionally'. In his *Discourse on Thinking* (in Heidegger and Krell, 1993) Heidegger suggests that there are two main kinds of thinking: *calculative* and *meditative*. Both are needed in their own ways. Calculative thinking is characterised by its serving of specific purposes and by its reckoning always with conditions that are given. Such thinking helps us to function in everyday life and to perform tasks. Calculative thinking is computational. There is currently a political preoccupation with measurable data, such as hospital waiting lists and school examination results. But, while figures are presented as hard facts, measuring can be a deceptive business, as the economist David Boyle (*Observer*, 14 January 2001) discloses in his exploration of 'counting paradoxes'. One such paradox is that when you count things they get worse. Among others, Boyle gives the example of increasing numbers of racist attacks reported after the 1998 public inquiry into the murder of the black teenager Stephen Lawrence in London. Another paradox is that if you count the wrong things you go backwards. Here Boyle cites the example of school league tables, introduced to promote competition and thereby improve standards. However, the pressure to raise standards may have led to schools excluding pupils whose results might bring their test results down.

Heidegger (in Heidegger and Krell, 1993) offers insight into calculative thinking when he tells us what it isn't, it 'never stops, never collects itself'. Heidegger continues:

> Calculative thinking is not meditative thinking, not thinking which contemplates the meaning which reigns in everything that is.
>
> (p. 46)

The Italian philosopher Corradi Fiumara (1992) suggests that there is a drawback to calculative thinking in the tradition of rationalism, which is:

> a propensity to render concepts increasingly abstract, thus leading to the disappearance of the multiplicity of relationships which had previously tied them to particular circumstances, and to their substitution with generalised relationships.
>
> (p. 12)

Meditative thinking serves a different purpose in human existence and perhaps we struggle more to understand its usefulness. It is more inclined to *being* than to *doing*. Heidegger suggests that meditative thinking requires greater effort. Delicate care and practice that need not be high-flown but which are available to us all. It is:

> enough to dwell on what lies close and meditate on what is closest, upon that which concerns us, each one of us, here and now, on this patch of home ground; now, in the present hour of history.
>
> (p. 47)

This pointing to the 'here and now' and the 'patch of home ground' is significant in a number of ways. It joins with the project of bringing philosophy out of the ivory tower of the academic world and into day-to-day living. Studying philosophy is worthwhile and so is the attempt to apply and test out philosophical ideas in daily life.

Both Heidegger and Fiumara allude, in different ways, to the significance of individual human experience. They also seem to point to ways of thinking that acknowledge the unique and vital context of ideas or experience as a counterbalance to methods that seek only to generalise and to suggest that broad categories and rules can always operate as guiding principles. What impact, if any, should these perspectives on thinking have on the educational tradition of truth seeking and critical thinking that have origins in Plato's Socratic dialogues?

## Living with contradictions

A vital feature of philosophy is its interest in rearranging, shifting, displacing and reframing ideas and beliefs. Another feature is its attempt to exist in places of uncertainty, exploration, possibility and imagination. Philosophising requires that assumed boundaries and freedoms should be questioned. There is no single way of achieving this. There are many paths to philosophical thinking and to the achievement of conceptual reframing. They include questioning by self or another, logical challenge and argument, reflection on personal experience and the use of humour and irony. Other approaches used with young people include exploring perspectives through story and comparative religious, historical or artistic study, 'experiential' approaches such as drawing, games, role-play, music, drama and meditation.

The introduction of thinking skills into the official curriculum is a double-edged sword. It is important to avoid formulaic procedures that become habitual. It is necessary to locate enquiry and dialogue firmly within the experience of the participants. One consequence of this approach is the need to give young participants greater responsibility for deciding the agenda and to question one's own power and authority as an adult, whilst retaining responsibility for the provision of care and education. How to carry out one's responsibilities is never permanently resolved and has to be given on-going attention.

The teaching methodology associated with the community of enquiry can provide entry into this transitional space with students. What is extraordinarily stimulating about this way of working is that it demands that teachers, and other adults, keep questioning their assumptions about knowledge and learning and what matters. If used as a formula it loses its strength. We gain nothing by seeing it as a programme that we can use to address political agendas such as the 'teaching of citizenship'.

# 5  Thinking, democracy and citizenship

Thinking skills have now become part of the official curriculum in many countries. Most teachers would probably want to claim that they encourage independence of mind, investigation and problem solving. The National Curriculum in England has, from its inception, made many references to enquiry, to hypothesis and testing, to planning and evaluation. So why the further emphasis on thinking skills again in the revised 2000 edition of the National Curriculum? What more is needed? Teaching thinking is a rather seductive and fashionable idea, a growing trend. The wary, the experienced and the healthily sceptical will rightly wonder what may lie behind the interest of government departments and policy makers in the inclusion of thinking in the formal curriculum. Will the teaching of thinking skills come under the influence of assessment trends and be formulated as an itemised tick list, and will the impetus generated by critical thinking enthusiasts be lost as a result?

The adoption of specific teaching techniques and methods that seek to improve children's thinking is not a new phenomenon. Like every other area of education, it has its various schools of thought. A very readable summary of different approaches can be found in Robert Fisher's *Teaching Children to Think* (1990). Broadly speaking, the teaching of thinking is considered in three different ways. Thinking skills programmes are based on taxonomies of transferable thinking skills. They follow an instrumental view of thinking where thinking skills are conceived of as tools or frameworks that can be developed discretely and applied in a range of contexts. They are often offered as activities that are enjoyable, challenging and refreshing for students, intending to provoke a departure from tired and unproductive learning habits. They are often used to try and bring about enhanced achievement and have been shown to achieve such success. The Somerset Thinking Skills programme is a good example of such a programme (Blagg *et al.*, 1988).

Secondly there is teaching that is carefully structured and organised to encourage particular kinds of systematic thinking. It adopts problem-solving, investigative and experiential approaches within the context of learning particular subjects. It promotes critical and creative thinking. An example of such practice that has had an impact on pupil achievement is Adey and Shayer's (1994) Cognitive Acceleration through Science and Maths Education. In this Piagetian approach the learning activity needs to be carefully designed to make particular demands on the student and to maximise opportunities for discovery and solving problems. There is strong emphasis on the teacher's role as a mediator whose in-the-moment question, modification or intervention can make a critical difference to the level of challenge and the reframing of understanding. Feuerstein's Instrumental Enrichment also puts tremendous emphasis on the role of the teacher as a mediator (see Fisher, 1990).

Finally there is the interest in thinking about learning that is expressed in the term 'meta-cognition'. It is argued that an added layer of thinking can be developed through explicit and deliberate attention to learning processes. As part and parcel of every learning situation, students are encouraged to be aware of their approaches to learning and to engage in discussion and reflection on how they learn. Attention is paid to reviewing the process of learning and considering how these processes may be applied in the future. The notion of teaching for meta-cognition is disputed by those who argue that all learning is situated. This argument implies that there can be no direct transfer of separated thinking tools from one situation to another, however explicitly drawn out.

## Distinctiveness of philosophy with children

Philosophy with children embraces both thinking skills and enquiry-based learning. Its learning context is most often created through carefully structured exploration of a variety of narratives found in story, myth, poetry, news, drama, music, painting, photography. Philosophical enquiry addresses the ground of meta-cognition as part of the ground of philosophy, which has always been concerned with the nature of mind, the nature of thought, the nature of knowledge and with issues of truth and reality.

Bringing the development of thinking and values together is a defining feature of the philosophy with children movement. Philosophy with children adopts a clear position with regard to the broader aims and purposes of education in a democratic society. Its stated political and social values are clear. The principles behind this approach to extending and improving children's thinking have been practised in many countries over more than thirty years. The approach originated in the United States with the work of Matthew Lipman and it sets out to influence the whole life of the school and its inhabitants. It seeks to broadly influence children's educational achievements and to make a positive contribution to schools as social communities.

## The roots of philosophical enquiry

The roots of this practice originate in a number of different philosophical traditions. Practitioners may emphasise different aspects of it according to their own beliefs and circumstances. It is associated strongly with Plato's teacher, the Greek philosopher Socrates, born in 469 BC. For Socrates the path to knowledge begins with the recognition of one's ignorance. The teacher's role can be compared with that of a midwife and the teacher must question in a way that allows the truth to be revealed. Like the midwife, the teacher assists in the birth of ideas.

The idea of a collaborative *community of enquiry* originates in the work of the American pragmatist philosopher Charles Peirce (1839–1914). He argues that we are participants, not spectators, in knowledge making. Knowledge is not a body of certainties but a body of explanations. John Dewey (1859–1952) believed in the application of co-operative intelligence and in learning as problem solving. Dewey argued that schools should be participatory communities, a meaningful part of society where young people could develop as citizens.

In the practice of collaborative enquiry we can also detect traces of critical theory, with its emphasis on the desirability of social transformation, reconstruction and the need for students to acquire critical languages and frameworks to analyse a wide variety of issues and to challenge existing power structures. Finally there is now a legal impetus to the notion of increasing participation for children in a wide variety of decision-making processes embodied in the UN Convention on the Rights of the Child.

The beliefs at the heart of critical and collaborative enquiry with children are drawn from philosophical, social, political, psychological and educational perspectives. In a democratic society the diverse and active participation of citizens is necessary to protect values such as human rights, individual freedom and equality. Children should be encouraged and given room to participate in society from an early age and in contexts that are meaningful to them such as families, schools and other settings where they have a stake.

The aims and purposes of education in a democracy are not only to provide training in basic skills to assure economic wealth for society but equally to address the problems and needs of daily life, in public and private domains. The participatory nature of a democracy implies a non-authoritarian form of moral education, since it implies that citizens must be self-regulating. Kelly (1995: 172) writes:

> In a democratic society, moral principles must be self-accepted rather than uncritically imbibed; they must be freely chosen rather than externally imposed; the democratic citizen must, in Kantian terms and in literal terms, give him or herself the laws he or she obeys. He or she must do this, however, in the light of an awareness of the collective 'good' of the community. Individualism must be tailored to communal responsibility.

Personal, social and moral education can be taught in ways that foster children's ability to regulate themselves. Autonomy and self-determination have been fundamental features in the work of a number of progressive educationalists with very different political, social and moral visions of the educational world.

Moral discourse and decision making have both intellectual and affective dimensions that have to be considered when devising a curriculum that incorporates philosophical enquiry. According to Jerome Bruner (1996) a curriculum is arguably at its most effective when it is 'participatory, proactive, communal, collaborative and given over to constructing meanings rather than receiving them'.

Bruner (1996) argues that schools are valuable because they are extraordinary places, 'for getting a sense of how to use the mind, how to deal with authority, how to treat others'. The 'stakeholder' status can be extended significantly in favour of children by providing them with opportunities to exercise responsibility and a chance to explore at least some parts of the curriculum in their own terms. Schools that adopt philosophical enquiry provide very fertile ground for this.

> The possibility of nurturing the 'reasonable person' lies at the heart of education in a liberal democracy. Reasonableness is more than rationality. Being reasonable is neither simple nor constant. Ethical precepts do not easily or automatically become praxis. They need exemplification in practice.
>
> (Bruner, 1996: 78)

Schools can capitalise on the fact that, from a very early age, children are capable of and interested in the rational, logical, intuitive and moral dimensions of thought and action. Schools have a wonderful opportunity to nurture children's thinking by placing high demands upon it and by awakening children to how they can use their intellectual and affective faculties.

## Counting children in: philosophical enquiry and citizenship

Philosophical enquiry with children, with its emphasis on oral work, narrative voice and inclusive, democratic practice, provides a powerful means by which children can listen to their peers, share experience and explore meaning. They can learn to express their views with confidence, knowing that their voices are heard and they can raise questions of interest and concern to them. Children come to understand how to take risks in their thinking and questioning. They realise they can do so within a safe structure and in an atmosphere of care and security. In this sense philosophy with children is one very good way of helping to promote and to exercise children's rights as citizens. Ideas of citizenship will almost certainly arise spontaneously as groups of children debate the rules of their engagement with each other. This could well include direct challenges to ways in which the authority of the school is deployed.

Western societies often demonstrate ambivalent responses to children's rights. I remember seeing a large poster in a French district court. It listed the many ways in which one could become a citizen of the republic. You could be born abroad to French parents, for example. But three-quarters of the way down the list, in a position that suggested ambivalence, was the statement that celebrating your eighteenth birthday would make you feel like a citizen. In keeping with many other countries, French children are not citizens.

The appropriateness of philosophy with children has been challenged by those who argue that children are developmentally incapable of the type of abstract and decentred thinking that they believe is required in philosophy. It has also been criticised by those who believe that children should be provided with a solid diet of basic education. Supporters of philosophy with children have met the challenge by providing evidence that children can do philosophy. This has been achieved partly by re-examining and reframing the very concept of philosophy itself (Kennedy, 1999; Murris, 1997). The theory and practice of philosophical enquiry with children continue to raise some fundamental questions about the nature of philosophy in the Western context and, in some cases, suggest a paradigmatic shift in our understanding of the creation of knowledge.

The experience of the communal dialogue which is the grounding practice of CPI [Community of Philosophical Inquiry] brings us face to face with the original condition of philosophy, philosophy not just as conversation, but as an emergent, multi-vocal and inter-active story about the world, and about persons thinking in the world.

(Kennedy, 1999: 96)

In his investigation of the nature of dialogue Kennedy refers to Winnicott's (1971) view of children's cognitive style, characterised by transitional subject–object relations, and drawing on both external life and inner reality. According to Winnicott children inhabit this transitional or potential space and negotiate it through all kinds of play. This space, in which children are accustomed but not expert, is also a space of creativity and dialogue.

Kennedy argues that the oral nature of philosophical enquiry is crucial to its radical role in our postmodern, written-information-soaked society. He claims that the historical devaluation of children's ability to reason is part and parcel of their assigned status as a politically inferior and disempowered group. Like other groups of people in society, such as women, ethnic minorities and the poor, children have traditionally been marginalised. Their claims to knowledge are devalued through a process that identifies them as *outsiders*. From such a position, children have a great deal to contribute to the work of deconstruction and reconstruction that typifies philosophical thinking and enquiry.

This book is not so concerned with the debate about whether or not children are capable of doing philosophy. It does offer examples of children's responses to their own questions and interpretations of their meaning or significance. It argues that children are not only able to participate in philosophical enquiry with one another, but they also have much to offer adults through their participation in philosophical conversation and communal dialogue. I have set out to explore the understanding and skills that teachers and other adults need to open up philosophical space with children, to enrich classroom thinking and conversation for children and adults alike, and to create knowledge.

# Part III

# Teaching through enquiry and dialogue

Chapter 6 seeks to identify obstacles to listening and the conditions that make listening possible in classrooms. It suggests that listening itself is a form of thinking and it demonstrates this through direct reference to classroom practice in managing rules.

- How does the adoption of rules of interaction hinder or help listening?
- How does a class move beyond rigid adherence to such rules?

Chapter 7 argues that teachers need to be conscious of ways in which the differential in authority in the classroom can obstruct recognition of children's perspectives. Listening to children implies respect for their ability to theorise and to draw on experience to inform their judgements.

- How can children's confidence to try out ideas be encouraged?
- What may teachers need to hold back in order to hear what children have to say?

Chapter 8 considers physical aspects of listening and concentration and describes some tried and tested methods of developing attentiveness and making transitions between different types of classroom activity.

- To what extent are practices of relaxation or meditation relevant to the teaching of thinking?
- Is philosophy a practical activity?

Chapter 9 begins with a discussion of ways in which philosophy allows us to question basic assumptions and to reconsider fundamental concepts. It suggest that we need to be cautious in deciding what is or isn't philosophical. It explores ethical and emotional dimensions of classroom philosophy.

- How do we know what is philosophical?
- What part do feelings play in doing philosophy?
- What ethical dilemmas might arise?

Chapter 10 challenges limiting expectations of how children may think or participate in discussion at particular ages, particularly when they are very young. It also questions the idea that all learning should take place in age or stage-related groups.

- Can very young children do philosophy?
- When may it be valuable to work in mixed age groups, including adults and children learning together?

Chapters 11 and 12 deal with different aspects of progression in philosophical enquiry. Chapter 11 shows how one particular enquiry in a junior class evolved over a series of sessions and suggests what progress was made. Chapter 12 shows ways teachers can record planning for enquiry and ways of monitoring progress.

# 6    Encouraging listening

Listening is central to any educational enterprise and teachers work hard, both at listening to children and at finding imaginative ways of encouraging children to listen to them. The Italian philosopher Corradi Fiumara argues it this way:

> Philosophical work is an 'effort' if listening is to be both accepting and critical, trusting and diffident, irrepressible and yet consoling. The coexistence of these irreducible contrasts is the very strength it anchors to.
>
> (1992: 90)

Vanessa, aged nine, a contributor to a community of enquiry in a primary school, recognises the desire of the teacher to listen impartially. She expresses her recognition like this:

> I like philosophy because I really like thinking and I can like share my thoughts with everybody, which I couldn't do at home because they would sort of like twist the words that I say.

We do not know enough about the conditions that make listening possible. When we want to encourage enquiry through dialogue we have to try and find out what the conditions may need to be. Listening can be a struggle. Listening is an embodied process but it is not just a case of activating the body's audio apparatus to hear what is being said. It is not just a matter of *decoding*. There have been occasions when we have all pretended to listen whilst our mind has been busy thinking of other things. Even when we try hard to give all our attention to listening it is inevitable that we will exercise some selectivity and make assumptions about what we have heard.

We bring our view of what is relevant to each and every act of listening and then project this on to the intentions of the speaker. In classrooms, where children are usually less powerful than adults and regarded as knowing less, teachers control much of what is heard and what is deemed relevant. A person's standing and authority influence the extent to which their voice is heard. Where children are involved in an examination of issues of authority, they need greater power and control in discourse than is usually available to them.

The majority of us find it easier to talk than to write. The gap between the ability to communicate orally and the ability to write and read is even greater for young children in the early stages of acquiring literacy skills. In classrooms, discussion will often provide the teacher with a different indication of pupils' thinking and understanding from that shown in a written task. It is for this reason, among others, that many teachers believe in the importance of providing time each week for extended discussion. A regular slot, in which there is no requirement for formal written work, also helps to give speaking and listening high status and to acknowledge that they are valued means of developing knowledge and understanding in their own right.

## Children making choices

As well as making room for discussion within the weekly classroom timetable, we can encourage involvement by giving children some choice in the focus and direction of discussion. Being allowed to choose boosts motivation and increases the chance that learners will be able to make contributions on the basis of their own experience. This, in turn, gives them more power. In talking about why they enjoy philosophical enquiry, children frequently report that simply being allowed to talk in an exploratory way is what they welcome. When this opportunity is established they will look forward to it eagerly and suggest topics for discussion, or ask to revisit something that has been the focus of a particularly lively debate. The excitement of a debate is palpable when children explore their chosen issues about whether dragons ever truly existed, how animals can communicate emotions, the implications of freezing human bodies for revival in the future, or how we know when we are dreaming.

One boy, a relative newcomer to philosophy class, put it like this. 'I like philosophy 'cos you can relax and just say what you feel like and it's a lot better so you can express yourself and your feelings.' His friend, also recently arrived from another school, added, 'It's interesting, you learn some new things and it gives you a chance to talk without everyone laughing and all that.' When pressed about why people don't laugh at each other's questions and comments in philosophy the first boy suggested, 'I think people don't laugh 'cos they all feel more relaxed and it's just easier to listen when you're relaxed.'

What is striking about these comments is that they seem to suggest that feeling relaxed, being free to explore ideas and feelings, and being encouraged to put forward questions for enquiry are an unusual experience for them. These children's feelings seem to indicate that making proper room in the school timetable for such activity is rather urgent.

Philosophical enquiry with children shows just how challenging and complex listening is for the teacher and the students. The task of active listening stimulates intellectual and emotional expansion. In a mature community of enquiry, members of the group begin to educate an inner voice. They increasingly engage in intra-personal dialogue. This developing skill of introspection and reflection benefits collaborative thinking and discussion with peers.

## Establishing rules to support listening and discussion

In many classrooms, rules for classroom talk are summaries of prohibition and restriction, rather than invitation, encouragement and guidance. The emphasis is too often on holding back, waiting, being invited by an authority figure. Rules often involve notions of fairness, forbearance, tolerance and submitting to the wishes of others. Much more rarely do they give advice about how to talk well and how good talking can promote good thinking. What is needed to encourage the development of rules to promote democratic discussion?

One starting point is to examine the usefulness (to everyone) of the rules that are in place. A rule that begins life as something simple and explicit can become a burden and something unnecessarily complex. The developing group soon learns to adapt to the needs of individuals and to the nature of different types of enquiry. Children learn to articulate their rules to newcomers and to explain the reasons for them in their own words without the teacher's prompting. As we work together the limitations of current rules are recognised by the group. New rules may need to be invented as the old rules begin to limit the group's effectiveness.

In the early stages of work with children the teacher will probably attend closely to the mechanics of listening and to the basic conditions it requires. Each class will devise its own guidelines for conducting enquiries. The list of rules is likely to include directives about sitting still, being quiet, avoiding interruption, taking turns, putting one's hand up before speaking. Box 1 shows a fairly typical response. Such rules are necessary to help establish the minimum conditions for discussion in a large group, especially when people are unaccustomed to collective enquiry and deliberation. When teachers invite children to offer suggestions for classroom rules, children may well recognise the current adult conventions of prohibition, couching their suggestions, as teachers often do, in terms of what not to do. Don't fidget, don't whisper to your neighbour, don't swear and be rude.

*Box 1*  Ground rules produced in the early stages of working as a community of enquiry

Don't shout out
When people are talking, don't talk over the top
We won't swear or use rude words
Be patient and wait your turn
Use self-control
Listen carefully with your ears, eyes and mind
Be still

It is instructive to clarify with the children why they think the rules need to be observed. This in itself provides rich material for philosophical enquiry and for exploration of group behaviour and dynamics. In a discussion which began with an exploration of why we encourage turn taking, for example, the children's discussion moved on to exploring the difficulty of *holding thoughts* in one's mind whilst waiting for a turn to speak. They asked, 'Is there a limit to the number of thoughts that a mind can hold?' 'What do thoughts look like?' 'Where do thoughts go when they are forgotten?' 'Can you have empty space in your mind?'

In the early life of a discussion group it seems to be helpful to remind children about the rules and guidelines at the beginning of each session. The group can choose to direct their effort towards keeping to one particular rule on each occasion. They can choose to make an effort to try:

- to explain and give reasons for your ideas;
- to follow on from the previous speaker;
- to make connections with other people's points.

Children can be invited to describe the details of the behaviour that they think the rule requires of them. They can be invited to describe what they find difficult. Taking turns is a good example to explore. Frequently, turn taking can be at odds with the call to make ideas follow on from one another. Rosy complains that Tim is waving his hand around while she is trying to speak and it is distracting her. The group make the decision that no hands must be up whilst someone is talking.

There is a classroom tradition, at least in British culture, that you must put your hand up to indicate that you want to speak in class or in a public meeting. Children soon become aware of the limitations of this procedure and can easily report them. Their arms ache from holding them up. They inadvertently, or mischievously, knock a fellow pupil on the head with a waving arm, causing a diversion or distraction. By the time their turn comes, they've forgotten what they wanted to say.

Over-rehearsing your argument before speaking publicly is a great source of inner disturbance. Children and adults alike can become too preoccupied with thinking about their own contribution to a meeting. They can be so distracted with thinking about their turn that they forget to listen to others. The ensuing contributions do not naturally link together and discussion can become disjointed.

There is a danger of adhering too rigidly to turn taking. Rather than being a fluent and unfolding dialogue, discussion remains just a series of individual responses, all of which are directed through the teacher or chairperson. This is not a 'meeting' of minds. It's important to ensure that the adopted procedures are understood. People need to genuinely accept them as working guidelines. It may become clear quite quickly that the current rules can be only provisional. Groups can grow and develop more sophisticated discussion by exploring the problems associated with inventing, adhering to and replacing rules.

The children have decided that turn taking and arm raising are problematic for their group. So how are we to know whose turn it is next? The children instruct the teacher to keep a running list that they can see. But we are still left with the problem of more sudden and urgent ideas that will not wait. How can we deal with these whilst ensuring that one or two more confident and articulate members do not dominate the group? If we adopt the passing round of a 'speaker's stone' there may be a temptation for some of us to pass it on to friends first. The teacher suggests that a special signal is needed to indicate that what follows is vital to the direction of the dialogue. She tells them about a mechanism she has come across in meetings. The children like the idea of 'red-hot cards' and everyone is issued with one. They may only be used once in a session and must be handed in after use.

Simply having the option of overriding the running order seems to create a sense of greater freedom. At the same time it appears to make each of us more responsible for the decision about whether what we want to say is *burning* or not. The teacher anticipates that on the first occasion there will be a rush of red-hot cards as the class enjoy the novelty. In fact, only one child makes use of his card. The group agree that he used it properly. Sandy puts her card up at one point. Then she hesitates and says, 'Actually I don't think it is urgent. Can I change my mind?'

When children are first given extended opportunities to pursue their own questions, they relish the chance to offer up their ideas. They are eager to take advantage of the space provided by the new rule. At this stage the pleasures of listening are subordinated to the need to be heard. As the children become more accustomed to the freedom of their own discussion the urgency to speak subsides and they can afford to listen to each other. The participants become so familiar with this way of working, so interdependent and collaborative, so interested in each other's ideas, so engaged with the questions in hand, that each example and counter-example has to be considered and weighed up.

The question of whether a hen could ever lay a cube-shaped egg becomes riveting as children bear witness to the different eggs they have seen. Many of the children live on farms. They can testify to some fairly extraordinarily shaped eggs. At this point the need of individuals to be heard appears subordinated to the collective fascination with the enquiry in hand. The shift can be transient, but it brings enormous pleasure and satisfaction when it occurs. When the more formally regulated discussion in the classroom comes to an end, the enquiry spills out into the playground. Terry says, 'I could do this philosophy all day!'

Reflection on rules helps to show their value and reduces the need for rigid adherence. Progress also seems to be made when children periodically review the use of the rules and their own success in using them. With infants, picture symbols to represent the rules can be drawn on a poster and displayed. This helps to jog memories during a session. A drawing of an ear stands for listening. A hand represents turn taking.

At the end of a session children are invited to comment on something they have found difficult or useful. They are encouraged to talk about something they feel they have achieved well, or something they have learned. After just a few weeks of working together, a group of five- and six-year-olds make a wide variety of evaluative comments about enquiry (Box 2 and Figure 4). There is clear evidence that they are noticing the behaviour and language that the teacher has decided to model for them. After reporting on their own concerns, the young

I was puzzling why the boy was allowed to take the dog out

*Figure 4* Anna's response to 'I was puzzling . . .' following KS 1 class discussion
of *Whistle with Willie*

*Box 2* Five- and six-year-old children's evaluative comments about what is
important when taking part in enquiry

'Keep your whole self still.'
'Look at the people when they're talking.'
'Don't go to the toilet in the story 'cos you miss some of it.'
'I did good listening today.'
'We could sort it out by sitting still and listening to each other.'
'I learned a lot . . . I can whistle' (after listening to the story
*Whistle with Willie* by Ezra Jack Keats (1977).

children in this group wanted to know what the teacher had learned
in the sessions of philosophy. She replied, 'I've learned how many
different ideas you have of your own.' 'I often do too much talking.' A
six-year-old girl showed insight into the teacher's role when she replied,
'But, Mrs P., you have got to talk to us to tell us how to do our work.'
These infant children showed considerable awareness of the purposes
and procedures that the teacher had introduced into the enquiry.
'I learned about agree and disagree . . . well, I haven't used those words

much before.' 'I learned how to be quiet and think.' 'Keep your innards quiet.' 'Some people helped me think of an idea.'

How often are classroom rules really seen from children's points of view? Older children are only too conscious of the effort they have to make on a daily basis at school in conforming to the norms of classroom behaviour. The approach to devising and reviewing rules in philosophical enquiry gives children permission to highlight the realities of this struggle because the rules themselves are open to question.

Terry initiated a lively discussion about his difficulty in holding back giggles, knowing that once he started it would be hard to stop. Who has not had the experience in school of being set off by a classmate, knowing that at any minute the laughter is going to burst out uncontrollably? Terry described this as his 'tanks overflowing'. Everyone recognised the metaphor. His classmates were quick to offer examples of when it had happened to them. The children were torn between the pleasure of this kind of laughter and the recognition of its potential for disruption. We agreed that on occasion the pleasure had to win out, but that we would also value ways of resisting the pull when necessary. They saw that it could be off-putting or upsetting for classmates too, especially if they were trying to say something important. They knew it could be distressing if making fun of a member of the class triggered laughter. The children took up the idea of 'using self-control'. They exchanged practical tips for applying it.

The more experienced children become and the more they are encouraged to review their own progress, as well as that of the group, the more they can identify goals for themselves. Debbie says she wants to improve her self-control and learn better how to stay steady. Liam says he is interested in thinking about different ways the group choose a question for discussion. Andrew has been struggling with the emotions of others disagreeing with him. He is often tearful if his ideas are challenged, and his goal is 'controlling his thoughts', although it seems more likely that it is his feelings he wishes to control. Andrew's worries highlight an oft neglected dimension of group discussion. The emotional needs of the individuals in a group vary with age and personality. Part of the work of every successful group is the exploration of the emotional needs of its members. This work needs to be done in an atmosphere of mutual respect and common faith in each other.

# 7   Respecting children's ideas

As well as needing to make space in the school curriculum for discussion driven by children's concerns and questions, careful thought needs to be given to the treatment of individual contributions in any single discussion.

Children's worries about other children disagreeing with them illustrate the significance that we all attach to 'not being laughed at'. The advice from children offered in Chapter 2 emphasises the need for teachers to give adequate time to each person who speaks. Adults need to avoid rushing in to fill the silence. We all need time to think, time to remember what it was we wanted to say and time to find the words to express our thoughts properly. This is especially true in the exploration of new or controversial and sensitive areas.

Children also refer to the need for acceptance. This is expressed by many children in terms of wanting to feel that it is safe to express themselves. Particularly when they want to put forward tentative, incomplete ideas. Debbie suggests, 'Give children more time to think, to explain things to the teacher and longer to say things.' Anna reminds us to let children say things to us and to avoid situations where they feel 'I'd better not say that.'

There is a further dimension to this notion of acceptance in the context of philosophical enquiry. It has to do with how a contribution is received. Is it seen as valid, relevant and worthwhile or is it dismissed as silly or off the point? To what extent can adults recognise children's epistemological authority? Is it always teachers who must decide what is relevant? If adults do not always know better, then how can they manage this in discussion with children?

When young children are given free rein in discussion they are inclined to be playful and exploratory and to try out ideas. The collaborators in a community of enquiry need to make the recipe up as they go along. They need the opportunity to throw things into the pot to see what happens. This is not the same as suggesting that anything goes. Victor Quinn (1997) writes eloquently of the need for the teacher to ensure that critical challenge, restraint and economy of expression are features of classroom discussion. Also to be avoided are those situations, so easily created, where children are striving to guess what is in the teacher's mind and where the teacher is dominating the thinking. Philosophical enquiry needs to retain a sense of adventure and depth as well as intellectual rigour.

## Teddy bears moving

A discussion began among the children in a class of infants aged four to seven arising from a story. The children had watched a video about the adventures of a teddy bear. Several children expressed puzzlement that a toy bear was shown, walking, climbing and moving its head. They said it was strange because teddy bears do not normally move. Four or five others then agreed. Bears do not normally walk, they argued. For a few minutes it seems that there is unanimity. They have dismissed the possibility of a toy moving. All of a sudden one girl takes another tack. She says, 'I disagree with Mandy because teddy bears, when you go out of your room, they can move.'

Daniel interrupts, 'It's not real, it's only a video.'

How should the teacher respond here? The points made by Anna and Daniel both contain promising seeds to be cultivated. But Daniel's tone is a little dismissive. The phrase *only a video* suggests closure rather than openness to further exploration. A decision is made to put Daniel's point on hold – 'Hang on a minute, Daniel' – and to encourage Anna to enlarge on her statement. Following the teacher's intervention Anna now adds, 'I think it's quite puzzling because they don't move when you're in the room.' The reason, according to Anna, is 'because they don't want you to know that they can move.'

Anna's point seems to encourage other children to report on other examples of toys being left in one place and turning up in another. There is a sustained passage of talk in which children alternate between relating incidences of their toys moving, explanations for these occurrences and counter-explanations. Points are no longer directed through the teacher each time and there is a sense of flow in the dialogue. This occurs as room is made for the children's experiences. As the children talk about not finding things where they left them it becomes apparent to the teacher that it is quite logical for them to wonder about this. Adults often tidy children's things away, even in space that is nominated as belonging to the children. Anna's comment also allows the group to consider that things may not be quite as they appear to be. This is just the kind of argument that has the potential to create a philosophical stance. It is her comment that opens up the enquiry, promoting speculation and argument.

The episode is not resolved. It moves from an exploration of appearance and reality, in which Daniel's earlier comment about what is and isn't real plays an important part. It becomes an investigation into the possible motives of bears that move secretly. Linda, who raised the initial question about the toy bear moving, informs the group that she is going to watch her own teddy bear more carefully from now on. She has been influenced by the discussion.

In relating this episode to student teachers, questions have been raised about the wisdom of pursuing Anna's point. One student expressed horror. She said she was a scientist. She could not contemplate a situation in which she would *not* want to ensure that children learned the truth of things. Children have to be told what is real. This, in itself, is a philosophical problem for teachers to consider.

## What calls for quality in discussion?

It can be regarded as a healthy sign of listening and a sign of the power of dialogue when participants change their minds, as Linda did. On the whole, young children seem to worry less about changing their minds than do adults. They do not appear to see it as a sign of weakness or the inability to hold a position. Rather it is a natural outcome of involvement in discussion. This openness and willingness to shift their thinking is to be welcomed, since new knowledge and understanding may result. There is, of course, a danger in this. Young people are regarded as particularly vulnerable to influence and persuasion.

Teachers need to be alert that some children may be able to assert undue influence in discussion. Victor Quinn (1997) is known for adopting an approach to teaching children which employs *provocation in role*. The purpose is to help children to practise resistance and to learn how to reject persuasively presented ideas and the views of adults who use intimidation. Quinn's approach involves teaching children to be logical and to maintain a critical stance under pressure. So it is a combination of resilience, courage and flexibility that is sought in philosophical enquiry.

In any group some will be more vocal than others, and it is pleasing when children themselves encourage the more reticent. This happened when one child said, 'I want to know what David thinks.' For some children it can be quite a while before they are ready to speak at length in front of the whole group. I can remember being told quite firmly by one girl that her little sister 'Doesn't really talk very much.' This seemed to hold true for some time. Four years on, this reticent child has become confident and articulate in philosophical enquiry. I make a point of explaining to children that being silent can also be a way of participating in the discussion.

Another girl was also quiet for a long time. When she spoke for the first time she spoke at length, with clarity and power. It was evident that she had been absorbing ideas and debating them internally. When she did finally speak the rest of the class were exceptionally attentive. Everyone was interested in what she had to say. It is also striking when children demonstrate that they are able to hold on to various threads in a discussion. One soon hears phrases like 'Going back to what Jemma said . . .'

## What place for silence?

> When I go away in my own world then it's nice and quiet and no one disturbs you or annoys you.
>
> (Caroline, aged eight)

> I like it when you tell us at the beginning to close our eyes and go somewhere and I just like to lean against something and just go somewhere, like go back to when I was at play group. . . . I like it specially when I'm in somewhere where it's completely quiet . . .
>
> (Kirsty, aged nine)

Children are often thought of as noisy, wriggly, fidgety, constantly on the move. Concentration spans, particularly those of very young infants, are said to be noticeably short. This is sometimes presented as a fixed developmental characteristic. However, anyone who has watched little children at play will know that they can become deeply engrossed for long periods. They can also remain quite still and attentive for prolonged periods of time. They easily demonstrate the falsehood of developmentally based arguments that attempt to set the limit of their attention as two, three or ten minutes. The critical issue for children and adults alike is the extent of the individual's engagement with the activity in hand.

Five-year-olds, six-year-olds and ten-year-olds show little difficulty in remaining attentive and engaged when they are discussing one of their own questions in philosophical enquiry. Whilst involved in thought and talk they sit for long periods of time, often expressing aahs of disappointment when the time comes to stop for lunch or playtime.

Increasing fluency and attention are good indicators that genuine dialogue is taking place. To achieve this, teachers have to learn to recognise the take-off points and to allow discussion to follow its own course, rather than imposing a planned structure or direction.

## Indicators of listening

There are a number of factors that appear to prevent listening in classrooms. It is easy to fail to recognise the imbalance of power that children experience in the compulsory schooling system. Teachers can be alerted to this by spending time in other teaching and learning situations. Poor conditions for discussion may lead to children being fearful and fragile at the prospect of being wrong, being different, or being mocked. Teachers may unwittingly put too much emphasis on assessment and convey the impression that only utterances that are completely formed are acceptable. The lack of time and sense of overcrowding of the curriculum pose problems for teachers. The imposition of over-rigid boundaries of relevance limits opportunities for discussion. Narrow curriculum objectives militate against good-quality exchange and development through dialogue.

If adults want to overcome some of these constraints they have to develop their practice in a number of areas. First we must express our faith in children's thinking and trust in their authority with regard to their own understanding and experience. We need to be available to listen and be prepared to heed what children say. Secondly, we have to recognise that we have the power to create better conditions in classrooms for children's dialogue. We can make room for it and learn to openly acknowledge its value. We can find ways of acknowledging the contributions that individual children make. We can accept that working on 'half-baked' ideas is fruitful. We can try to see things from the children's point of view by asking them to share their views publicly. Finally, so it does not begin to sound like a series of do's and don'ts, we have to learn to make more use of responsiveness and intuition. These are invaluable in knowing when and when not to intervene in discussion. They help us to heed critical stages in the development of any group.

Teachers play a vital role in empowering children by creating metadiscourse. This can be achieved through the injection of comments and questions that draw children's attention to features of their thinking and to the bigger picture of an on-going enquiry. At the conclusion of an enquiry, teachers can direct the children to the processes and general consequences of discussion by asking:

'Have you been influenced by anybody's ideas today?'
'What's made you change your mind?'
'Have you noticed any new thinking in the group?'
'Were you able to concentrate or were you distracted?'
'Did this discussion link with any others that we've had?

Practice at listening to and joining the meta-discourse that the teacher creates helps children to make connections between apparently disparate parts of the enquiry. It also encourages them to practise reviewing and helps the skill of summarising. It signals that winning or losing an argument is not highly valued for itself by emphasising that there is value to be gained by exploring the process of argument, engaging in thinking and by introducing new ideas.

## Listening in open-ended enquiry and dialogue – qualities to strive for:

Children need to be confident that:

- Their accounts of their experiences and their opinions will be treated with respect and accepted as valid.
- Teachers will be faithful to the detail of their contributions.
- They will be given time to speak.
- They will not be mocked or humiliated.
- They can be tentative, playful or exploratory in their thinking.
- They can change their mind if they want to.
- Minority views will be supported.
- Challenges to the *status quo*, when raised as part of the process of enquiry, will not be punished.

Teachers need to make the effort to:

- Be open-minded and encourage openmindedness.
- Be willing to reconsider established ideas and to view facts, ideas and theories as provisional.
- Be supportive when there is a struggle to articulate new ideas.
- Allow proper time for each person's contribution.
- Be skilled in recognising connections between ideas.
- Hold back on their own interests in any enquiry.
- Check for possible misunderstandings.
- Be flexible, intuitive and responsive to the dynamic of a discussion.

Listening is not a mechanical decoding skill. It is a complex and problematic aspect of communication and thinking. Teachers need to consider:

- The nature of schooling, the views of knowledge that are presented, the seat of power and authority in the school context.
- Listening is thinking; as we listen we make all kinds of judgements and choices.
- The levels of distraction in school that obstruct listening.
- The many claims, such as those of parents, the wider public, the government, pupils or the teaching profession that can impinge on the responses that teachers can make to pupils.

# 8 Relaxing, meditating and being silent

The capacity for concentration, contemplation and attentiveness is something that can be cultivated deliberately by the teacher. Silence in school is not usually associated with personal liberty for the pupil. It is more often associated with formal, didactic teaching, with the imposition of adult authority, and sometimes with punishment. But only a generation ago silence was extensively imposed within schools. Pupil talk, when invited, often took the form of chanting and repetition.

In the context of a very rigid system in which there was virtually no individual privacy, it is perhaps not so curious that, at least for some pupils, the frequent and long periods of enforced silence actually offered some respite and freedom from externally imposed authority and austerity. The imagination could remain at liberty. The mind itself had privacy.

Nowadays books and courses about teaching stress the importance of verbal interaction. Teachers are expected to converse with children and, in turn, the children are encouraged to talk to each other. Group interaction is generally seen as vital in the development of children's knowledge and understanding. Carefully focused teachers' talk and teacher–pupil conversations are both regarded as vital in promoting learning in the classroom. Much of this book is dedicated to the importance of learning through speaking and listening in the classroom. In this it is not out of step with a general emphasis on the use of discussion. So it may be timely to review the purpose and value of silence. Rather than the silence imposed on children as part of a formal and authoritarian school regime of a generation ago, let us consider whether silence can contribute to the development of children's freedom of thought.

I want to suggest that silence provides an opportunity to support the thinking process, reflection and personal expression. Silence, and other techniques for stilling the mind and improving concentration, are valuable in their own right and for improving the quality of verbal interaction.

'Make your bodies still and ready to listen' is a settling phrase that I have used at the beginning of sessions with infants. On such an occasion one child said that, to really listen, you may have to be still inside your body as well as outside your body. This comment led to a discussion of what it might mean to be still inside as well as still outside. From this point the original phrase was adapted and became 'Make yourselves still, outside and inside.'

The control of internal movement and stillness continued to be a source of interest during philosophical enquiry as well as at other times in the classroom. Alan, a six-year-old, said you couldn't be completely still inside because your blood was circulating and your heart was beating and you couldn't stop that.

During another activity in the classroom Linda was once heard to urge a fellow pupil, 'For goodness' sake, David, keep your innards quiet.' These responses from the children indicate that it is worth giving much more thought to the business of beginnings and appropriate preparation for sustained discussion.

Many teachers attend yoga or meditation classes and attest to the benefits in helping busy individuals manage their lives. When teachers explore the uses of silence and relaxation in teaching it is often in the context of discovering or rediscovering them for their own well-being. It is worth considering the need that children have to relax, to be calm and inwardly refreshed. Teachers can begin by just giving children the opportunity to be still, to shut out unwanted external noise and fuss and to turn inward, to become calm.

Including silent relaxation at the beginning of periods of dialogue is to be recommended. This suggestion is based largely on practical considerations. The pace of classroom life can be fairly hectic and fragmented. There are few opportunities for classroom activity that promote contemplation, yet we are often seeking a thoughtful response from children, not only in poetry sessions but also in PE, assembly and circle time.

Explicit classroom practice can help those children who do not know what steps to take to quieten themselves. It is foolish to think that all noisy children prefer to live their lives in an agitated and disruptive state. Wanting to be quiet may need to be followed by being taught explicitly *how* to be quiet.

Careful attention to posture makes for more sustained comfort and less distraction through discomfort. Physical relaxation can create a feeling of calm, well-being and preparedness. This could start as part of PE sessions, before being introduced into other lessons. An interlude of silence provides everybody with recovery time, from performance and from one another, and can ease the transition from one mode of working to another. Guided relaxation can bring about improved awareness of mind and body states. Periods of eyes-closed silence make it possible to 'watch' one's own thoughts. Knowledge and skill in physical and mental relaxation promote healthy self-maintenance, greater self-control and personal autonomy. Regular relaxation practice can contribute to the development of mindfulness and meta-cognitive ability.

Thinking in a community of enquiry demands certain behaviour from participants and explicit attention needs to be paid to creating the conditions for it. It can do no harm and children can simply take time out for themselves if they do not wish to take a full part in the suggested activity. This may lessen the potential for disruptiveness with some agitated children. It certainly helps others to develop their thinking skills and personal awareness.

Teachers do not need specialist training. There are plenty of books and tapes about relaxation techniques. Yoga offers approaches to physical relaxation, to breathing and meditation, and the techniques can be adapted for use with children. Many children will already be familiar with meditative techniques arising from religious and cultural practices. Others may regard the practice as taboo. What is important in the classroom is to make use of observation and feedback from children to modify practice until it suits the purposes of the class.

The idea of meditation is rarely new to the older children. In one class that was getting started with meditation, many of the children slightly cheekily imitated the classic yogic pose of legs crossed, hands resting upturned on the knees and first finger and thumb touching. When asked how they knew about this position, television was the answer.

One of the contexts in which they are most likely to be encouraged to try these things out is in the realm of sport. Footballers, athletes and other competitive sportsmen and women are now being trained in mental preparation techniques, including visualisation, because it enhances their performance. Trainers promote such exercises because they can increase one's belief in success. They reduce anxiety and help harness energy and concentration, focusing them on the desired goal. Physical education seems to be in the forefront in terms of recognising the need to achieve an integrated approach to the instruction of body and mind.

One popular children's television programme has shown a British record-breaking strong man using visualisation in a training session with a group of runners of all ages. He asks them to shut their eyes and imagine themselves winning the race.

## Children's responses to relaxation and meditative practice

The first time I invited the infant group to 'meditate' I wanted them to feel safe and comfortable. I used a visualisation practice that is a common relaxation exercise. I told them that in our minds we could go to a place where we felt safe. We could imagine the safest of all places. We might find a loved object, perhaps a toy or a teddy. I asked them to focus on the object and to imagine touching it and holding it. For the older children, I adapted this exercise by inviting them to go to their favourite place, either real or imagined, and to remain there for some moments.

This proved very popular. Each time we met the children would ask me, 'Can we go to our favourite places?' Afterwards they would want to talk about their favourite places, and for some children this time had a truly blissful quality about it. The silence was very enjoyable. The infants had little difficulty with this activity although one or two older children seemed to find it almost impossible to shut down. Perhaps it felt too risky to keep their eyes closed.

On occasion I used guided relaxation, and this offered greater structure. I used the phrase 'I want you to take your mind to . . .' (and then named parts of the body in turn: your toes, the soles of your feet). On one occasion this prompted a discussion that just took off and at the end of the session no one wanted to go home. Jenny said that as I spoke she saw little tiny men going from one part of her body to another. She said that for as long as she could remember, and certainly since she had been able to speak, she had been able to visualise little people in this way.

This exercise led to a discussion about the experience of knowing. Whether knowing is local or general. Whether it is wholly in the mind, in the brain, or whether one can 'know' with one's skin, with one's stomach. At another level it was to do with making assumptions. Can we assume that one person's body is made in the same way as another's? If we look inside one body and fail to see 'little men', can we be sure that the same will be true of all bodies? Another part of the discussion was to do with an individual's right to hold certain beliefs and whether at a certain point one should simply agree to differ.

It engaged the children in a remarkable and sophisticated discussion about what they considered to be acceptable levels of challenge to another person's views and the appropriate ways for such challenges to be expressed. They described how much disagreement they could manage, what pressures their self-confidence could tolerate and the boundaries of mutual respect in argument.

## Starting points for silent relaxation in the classroom

A comfortable sitting posture is important, and a balance needs to be struck between suggesting a position and allowing the children to find one that suits them. As with most new approaches, more guidance is required in the early stages. Each child needs a clear space so that they are not touching anyone else. I ask them to make sure that they can breathe deeply and keep their spine erect to allow the lungs to expand. I suggest they check that particular parts of the body are relaxed. 'Are your arms and hands loose?' 'Are your shoulders unshrugged and mouth relaxed? 'Is your forehead smooth?' I look around and make sure that each person looks comfortable and I remind them that we are going to be sitting as still as possible for several minutes. When all preparation is done and the hum of shuffling is over, eyes can be closed. I also close my eyes. I talk continuously at this point because it is a surprising leap for a large group to move from seeing awareness to blind contemplation. The encouragement comes from the privacy of these few moments. I invite the children to put away their worries and frustrations and to enjoy this little bit of time to themselves. I ask them to close the doors and to look inside, not outside. Sometimes we take a few deep breaths at this point, to release tension and to move towards more effortless physical stillness. I open my eyes so that I can quietly give encouragement to anyone who is struggling to be still.

## Ideas for inward looking

I have tried a number of ideas for extending these minutes of quietness with children. Mostly these are small journeys of the imagination, designed to invoke a sense of pleasurable calm and serenity. Each journey is punctuated by periods of total silence, and the length of these periods can be built up gradually.

> Imagine you are in your favourite place. Somewhere that you feel safe and happy. It could be somewhere real, like a room in your house, or a place outside in a garden, park or field. You may be with somebody or you may be by yourself. It could be an imaginary place. When you decide where it is I want you to try and bring it to mind in all its detail. Notice all the colours and shapes and sounds. What does it feel like to be in that place? What is good about it? Now can you try and hold it very still? Imagine you are floating on a Li-lo on very calm water. It's a beautiful warm day and the sun is shining. You can see birds flying above and you can

hear the water lapping very gently. Your body is quite floppy and sleepy on the Li-lo. You are enjoying the rocking motion. [Older children like this one.] What if you were to create your very own den? It can be made of any material you like. It might be up in a tree or somewhere in your house or garden. It might be in an imaginary place. See if you can picture it in your mind's eye. What does it look like outside? Is there a secret entrance? Imagine that you have made your dream den and that you go inside. Imagine you are holding an object or a toy that you are especially fond of. It might be a teddy, a doll or a cuddly toy. It might be a beautiful stone or shell. It might be a little toy car or figure. It could be a model that you've made. Try to remember exactly how it feels to touch and hold it. Is it soft or hard? Is it smooth and shiny, scratchy and rough, hard-edged and cold, or furry and fluffy? Look at all the detail and hold it as still as you possibly can. [Younger children like this one.] Imagine taking a journey around your body. Take your attention to your feet to begin with. Think of each of your toes, your toenails, the tops of your feet, the soles of your feet, the bones in your feet, your ankles. [Continue or begin with other parts of the body.] Imagine you are on the top of a very high mountain. You are so high up that you can see for miles around. You are so high up that you are almost touching the sky. It is completely quiet and the air is still. Nobody can bother you here. Nobody can tell you what to do.

Each of these has provoked different reactions from children. They often want to talk about the content of their journey. Sometimes we do discuss mental visualisations and they will often lead into a philosophical enquiry. Sarah said that she often uses this time to pretend she is Annie and that is who she is going to be when she grows up. Other children use the time in their own way, and this is accepted. The exercises are offered to the children but they are under no obligation to take them up.

Louis and Sarah complained about the last of the ideas listed above. They said they never liked being completely alone and that they preferred somebody else to be there at all times.

Handbooks on meditation provide a number of exercises using the breath to focus attention and to empty the mind of thoughts. Children can begin by noticing how deep sighs help them to relax the body at the start of a quiet time. They can distinguish between using the nose and the mouth and filling different parts of the lungs. The exercises usually involve counting the breath in different ways, or trying to maintain a focus on the inward and outward flow from one particular point, such as the entrance to the nostrils. This counting and watching absorbs attention and creates a rhythm that induces a calm concentrated state. It is not easy to achieve. A balance has to be found between making an effort but not trying too hard.

Sometimes there is giggling and loud sighing and yawning. It is a grand opportunity for mischief like nudging and poking and trying to distract your neighbour. I know the pleasure of such giggle-making moments myself and I don't take much notice, but I invite the children to see whether they are able to ignore it and concentrate on their own thoughts. They have described all kinds of ways of ignoring interruptions and are proud of their ability to use self-control.

After we have held at least a minute of silence I invite the children to gently come back to the room in which we are sitting and to show me that they are ready and prepared to work by opening their eyes again. Some of them love to take their time over this. There is always a noticeably calmer and more relaxed atmosphere. They often remark that they didn't want to come back and that it wasn't long enough. If I don't offer a relaxation they will often request one. Clive and Tim have both commented that they notice a link between their success in achieving a state of relaxation at the beginning and their ability to concentrate and take part properly in the remainder of a session of enquiry. If they are unable to relax they often find it hard to settle and listen to each other.

I asked the children whether they ever tried this relaxation technique at other times. One or two said they had when they found themselves alone in a room at home. Several of them said they had tried it but it was difficult on your own. This is also my experience, and the group setting is paradoxically both a distraction and a support.

## Development of a single theme over several sessions

An alternative approach to the imaginary journey is to focus on an object and to use the mental reconstruction of it to try and hold the mind in one place. This can be developed over a number of separate occasions. Objects such as stones, shells, fir cones, pieces of wood or fabric are suitable for the exercise.

For the first session I took to school our family collection of stones collected from many walks in different places. I put them in a wooden bowl and passed them around the circle, so that each child could take one. I asked them to hold the stone and to examine it, noticing its shape, colour, size and pattern, texture, temperature and weight. I asked them to close their eyes and try to reconstruct the image of the stone in their mind. I asked that they try to hold the image very still. Each time the mind wanders off, bring it back to the stone. We had three minutes of complete silence. Success in the suggested task is almost irrelevant. The effort is intriguing and the children enjoy reporting on what has happened behind their eyes. Tariq said his stone was surrounded by blackness. Neil said his stone was turning round. Louis's stone became an enormous boulder. The first time we used the stones, several children rolled them, threw them a little way into the air and passed them from hand to hand, playfully.

In the second session I put the stones out on a tray woven from sisal. It is a rectangular basket shallow enough to allow all the stones to be clearly seen. I said that before giving them the stones I wanted a contract with them. They were to be the keeper of the stone for a short time and during that time the stone must not lose contact with their hand. If they dropped, threw or rolled it the contract was broken and the stone would be returned to the tray. I wanted them to hold the stone still for a while and not play with it during the period of stillness and silence. I called children to come and see if they could recognise their stone on the tray. Most of the children collected a stone, immediately recognising the one they had used previously. A few changes had to take place when identity was mistaken. I reminded them about the contract they had made as the keeper of the stone. This scenario lent a rather serious and mystical quality to the occasion, which encouraged responsibility and achieved greater stillness. The quality of the silence was different, in that it seemed more effortless and it was maintained for nearly five minutes. I ended it and noticed many children had been very absorbed by the meditation. Some smiled when they opened their eyes as if returning from elsewhere.

In the third session I left the stones at home. The children asked if I had brought them as soon as we began. I said I wanted them to look at me and see if they could read my mind. I sat myself in the position ready for meditation. As each child adopted a similar position, I told her or him they had succeeded in reading my mind. Kevin was still fidgeting. I said there was one more thing in my mind he needed to read. He stopped fidgeting and I said, 'You read my mind. How did you do that? What was I thinking?' He replied, 'You were thinking "Keep still".' I said it was remarkable that he could read my mind like that. This was both playful and a way of engaging the children with the idea of different forms of communication and the nature of the mind. It breaks the tedium of always repeating the same set of instructions.

When their eyes were closed I asked them to imagine coming to the tray, looking for their stone, finding it, picking it up and sitting down with the stone in hand. I asked them to remember its shape, coldness, smoothness or roughness and to hold it steady in their hand. 'Now can you make a picture of it in your mind and hold it steady like you did before?'

The visualisation was concluded when they returned the stone to the tray. Some children said that the image was just as vivid but others found it difficult. During the silence one boy had been extremely distracted. He had continued to make noises and had briefly left the room. He recovered his composure when he came back. I was struck by how little reaction this provoked from the others. I asked them how they felt. Linda said that when we first started she thought there was no way she would manage to concentrate today. But she had succeeded and felt relaxed. Jenny said that she had bitten her tongue gently to stop herself from laughing. Others said they had made a conscious effort to remain still and keep their eyes closed. Their self-control was remarkable.

Session four took place in December. The previous Sunday, the children had taken part in a Christingle service in the local church in which all those present had held a lighted candle wedged in an orange. The lights had been turned off while we sang a carol. The flames had lit up the faces of young and old as they stood in a circle, bringing a hint of warmth to the freezing air in the old stone building. I took a candle to the class, thinking that we could use the flame as the focus for our meditation. It was Friday afternoon and the end of a week of Christmas plays. The class was tired and fidgety and it was hard to persuade them to settle. I persisted and lit the candle, suggesting they begin by looking at the flame. They could close their eyes when they thought they could hold the image without looking. We tried to be silent. It was a struggle, and remarkably some children achieved it. I saw one boy trying to distract his neighbour by blowing towards his cheek. It was in vain. Adrian remained still and didn't open his eyes. Afterwards he said he imagined a hand pushing the air away and that he kept bringing the flame to mind to maintain his concentration. Those who had managed to remain still and focused had used the candle flame in one way or another. I did not succeed at all on this occasion, and the remainder of the session was a struggle for me as I wondered whether to abandon our philosophical discussion or to persist.

Session five took place on the last day of the winter term. It was a Friday morning, first thing. I set the challenge of our longest-ever silence. Could we manage five minutes without any prompting whatsoever? Kevin asked, 'Can we read your mind?' I agreed, and they all used this as a signal to prepare for the meditation. Within seconds they were sat ready to begin. I asked Daniel, who was often disruptive, if he could make me a Christmas present of his effort on this occasion. He did. Compared with his most familiar behaviour, he was much more attentive and needed reminding only once during the whole session. It felt like a breakthrough. I reminded the children that those who managed last week had relied on the candle flame to keep them on track. There followed an effortless four and a half minutes of silence and stillness. The school secretary opened the door and asked if could she interrupt for a minute, apologised when she saw what we were doing and withdrew. The children did not move. We continued for another minute. In review, they described variations on the flame that they had seen. Some heard imaginary voices telling them to keep going when a distraction arose. They appeared to be gaining various techniques for maintaining self-control and persisting in the face of distractions. The infant teacher in the room next door said she had been envious of our peacefulness when she looked through the window and saw us sitting around the candle.

## Aspects for the teacher to consider

Practice improves this experience. Some children take to it very easily and others need a great deal more attention and encouragement. The teacher needs to find or invent the language that seems fitting. Statements like 'Let go of your worries,' 'Take your attention inwards,' 'If you get distracted, just let it pass and start again,' 'Notice what's going on in your mind,' 'What do you see inside there?' are the sorts of guiding phrases that I use. They are intended to bring about a quality of attention that is concerned with the immediate present. This promotes peaceful concentration that is self-orientated and that enhances self-awareness. The activity provides material for discussion of meta-cognition.

I try to model the kind of posture and disposition that I believe is useful. I have learned to break the activity down into smaller steps and to talk a class through those steps one by one. The tone of voice and the pace of speech need to be modified to suit this activity. Patience and humour need to be cultivated.

## Is it really meditation?

The term *meditation* may be used to describe a variety of practices. Different groups and individuals who are well versed in meditation may draw distinctions between the activities described above and the practice of meditation. Meditation may include guided imagery, quiet moments of contemplation and silence, breathing and relaxation techniques. For some practitioners there is a strong spiritual dimension and an ideal towards which one is aiming. I use the term 'meditation' in an inclusive sense. To meditate means to think deeply and quietly and to plan one's mind. In some cases, it works to stimulate and clarify thinking and in others it encourages a mental state which is beyond thought and which reaches towards a state of restfulness. David Fontana (Fontana and Slack 1997: 5) describes the practice as:

> essentially a state of poised directed concentration, focused not upon a train of thoughts or ideas, but upon a single clearly defined stimulus . . . as the opposite of wandering thoughts or even a directed train of thinking . . . it is a very special kind of sitting quietly doing nothing, in which the mind is held clear and still, alert and watchful, and free from losing itself in thinking.

I have decided to use the word 'meditation' with the children in order to pave the way for the discussion about what it means to different people and to enable them to make their own way with it. My intention is that we should explore it together and share our experience of its potential, its difficulties, its limitations and the uses we make of it. I think that each of the children can add to what is known about it.

In the introduction to his book David Fontana points out that adults introducing children to meditation need to show sensitivity. He argues that it should be offered in a non-prescriptive way, not imposed, and that young people must be free to judge its usefulness and to accept or reject meditation accordingly. His book provides excellent guidance on meditation with children of all ages and is essential reading for any teacher who wishes to be well informed and who wishes to adopt a well grounded approach to this ancient practice.

## Meditation as part of discourse

It is still common in Western culture to adopt a perspective in which body and mind are seen as separate entities. So influential is this way of thinking that it is sometimes difficult to appreciate that such a perspective is neither universal nor infallible. Many traditional Eastern philosophies treat mind and body as inseparable. Lakoff and Johnson (1999) argue that recent developments in our knowledge of the brain and in cognitive science appear to confirm that consciousness and thinking are embodied processes. The architecture of the brain and of our sensory organs structures our ways of seeing, hearing and knowing.

Classroom activities are categorised as practical or non-practical. Such titles may also infer a certain status in the hierarchy of school subjects and knowledge. The philosopher is often painted as a person alone, engaged in lofty cerebral activity. However, philosophy can be viewed as a practical activity whose practice is collaborative and collective rather than individual. In the latter view, there is equal concern with the behaviour of the participants, the rules of discourse and social interaction as there is with the ideas that emerge. Doing philosophy in the classroom is an activity in which as much attention needs to be paid to the physical and emotional dimensions of thinking, listening and talking in a group, as to the skills of reasoning and argument.

## Philosophy as a practical and physical activity: elements to consider

The body:

- Build in time for the transition: think about including silent times, relaxation or visualisation activities to promote concentration.
- Make sure children are comfortable and can remain so: pay attention to seating, ventilation, etc.
- Include opportunities for movement and changes of pace, for comfort, for concentration and to provide interludes.
- Make sure that the seating arrangements allow everyone to see each other.
- Allow children to develop stamina for longer periods of concentration.

Interaction:

- Let children have time to think alone, time to talk to one other person and opportunities to work in a small group.
- Encourage children to address their comments to everyone in the whole class group, rather than direct them through the teacher.
- Hold back as much as possible once children have become accustomed to whole-class discussion: resist the urge to comment on every contribution.
- Include children in recording ideas in different ways, visually and graphically.

Activities:

- Have paper and pencils, Post-its, large felt-tips, large sheets of paper and board markers available for everyone to use as the need arises and remember to ask whether anything else is required.
- Incorporate drama and enactments of dialogues, either as starting points or ways of representing different viewpoints.
- Devise structured activities for individuals, pairs and groups at appropriate points or as follow-up: these might include drawings, writing dialogues, brainstorms, making mind maps and webs of ideas, writing and sorting questions, devising criteria for classifying ideas, Venn diagrams, lists, playing a thinking game.

# 9   Feeling for the philosophical

> I like philosophy because I really like thinking and you've got the feeling
> that people are caring about you and listening.
>
> (Julie, age 9)

> If a teacher teaches philosophy I think it helps her, not just the people
> that she's teaching . . . it helps her to understand how the children feel
> and what they're like and why they think like that.
>
> (Carolyn, age 10)

> Adults are expected to create spaces and promote processes to enable
> and empower children to express views, to be consulted and to influence
> decisions.
>
> (UNICEF, taken from unicef.org 1999)

Many fundamental ideas are part and parcel of our day-to-day thinking,
to such an extent that they are taken for granted. Such assumptions may
be necessary for us to function in everyday conversation. But in philosophy, everydayness is examined. We tend to juxtapose concepts such
as *mind* and *body*, *feeling* and *thinking*, *emotion* and *reason*, *subjective*
and *objective*, *self* and *outside self*. And this juxtaposition has structured
our experience, our understanding and our knowledge.

Although this dualism has been challenged from both scientific and
philosophical perspectives, it continues to exert influence and to shape
our ways of looking at the world. It influences the questions we ask
and those we don't ask. Philosophical enquiry offers opportunities to
reconsider the most fundamental questions and rules governing our
beliefs.

At this moment in the history of philosophy, children may be in
a special position to contribute to this endeavour (Kennedy, 1992).
The history of thinking shows us how philosophy thrives upon great
leaps. These great leaps have been prompted by discoveries in science
and by economic and social changes.

One of the intriguing aspects of philosophising with young children is that some of the taken-for-granted notions that tend to inhabit our beliefs and our discourses are not so firmly set in children's minds. It is partly for this reason that children's questions can strike some adults as naive. We can be too dismissive and lose the chance to see the horizons that children's contributions offer.

One of the arguments of this book is that dialogue can often be enriched when an adult is willing to join in with children's perplexity. Exploring the apparently obvious is valuable when it is of interest to the children to do so. We may not be able to experience the perplexity as children do, at the outset of an enquiry, but what is important is that we make room for children to be part of the process of determining what is and what is not philosophical.

This chapter discusses the responsibility and sensitivity that adults need to show with respect to children's ideas. It looks at what is needed to recognise the strength, wisdom and vulnerability that arise from youthfulness and comparative inexperience in the world.

## Making more room in philosophy for children's questions

What sorts of questions are allowed? In the literature about philosophy with children quite a lot has been written about what makes a question philosophical (Gardner, 1996; Lipman, 1997). There has been a lot of guidance written that seeks to help adults who are themselves beginning the adventure of trying to recognise a question that has philosophical potential. Do questions such as these that were asked by four and five-year-olds belong in philosophy or not?

> 'How do cats kiss?'
> 'Why do men have nipples?'
> 'How are rivers made?'

How may we explain to young children the decisions we make about where questions belong? After all, even the subject boundaries themselves have philosophical roots.

Once learners have acquired a sense of the boundaries of the disciplines of human knowledge, through their experience or through schooling, their questions tend to define the nature of their enquiry at the outset. There is an implicit sense of the kind of response that they are seeking. It may be a scientific explanation, a religious interpretation, a commonsense answer. Often, five-, six- and seven-year-olds have no idea of what it is to make a historical, scientific or linguistic enquiry. They are not subject-bound. Their questions do, however, present the educating adult with choices, sometimes difficult ones. The boundaries that we choose for the enquiry determine what we can do with the question.

When young children are starting out in philosophy, what they understand is that the community of enquiry is a place where they are encouraged to formulate questions about the things that puzzle them. They are helped in the process of turning a puzzled response into a question. They come to realise that we can make all kinds of use of our mystification.

Children come to understand that the enquiry offers a space and time where their questions matter and where they learn to put puzzling ideas, thoughts and feelings into words. Significant questions have genuinely arisen from that searching part of ourselves. It is not relevant at this point that others have asked similar questions before. Learning to recognise and sustain a state of perplexity is fundamental to the task of philosophy.

We should try to avoid being hasty when deciding the nature of children's questions. Karin Murris (1997) argues that it is not the question itself but the context in which the question is asked and the intention of the questioner that matter. We need to know something about the origin of a child's question and a little about why it has been asked.

It is useful to demonstrate the methods by which we categorise different types of knowledge and enquiry. We cannot usually explain abstract philosophical theory to children but we can try to show in practice how philosophy has treated questions in particular ways. So it is helpful not to reject questions out of hand as non-philosophical but to investigate where they come from and how they may be linked with philosophical ideas. The teacher can indicate to children the different ways that a scientist, an artist or a philosopher may approach questions.

## Being philosophical also exercises the emotions

Philosophical enquiry seeks to maximise involvement and motivation. Thinking, listening and talking are activities that involve body, heart and mind. In schools, where it is included in the curriculum, we talk about *doing* philosophy, just as we talk about doing mathematics and physical education. This philosophy is practical and wholly absorbing. This philosophy is a way of life.

One sign of success is the level of active participation and engagement with ideas. Children do not need to be managed by the adult because they are too busy discussing something that matters to them. They become motivated when obstacles or prerequisites are removed. They are able to think more productively when adults avoid imposing unnecessary rules and rigid controls. Children's interest is heightened when they care enough.

Maintaining engagement whilst helping to extend and deepen the enquiry puts the adult in a demanding and rewarding role.

### Philosophical feelings

In a classroom community of enquiry, the affective dimensions of philosophical practice are quite evident and are intertwined with the cognitive process. Children experience perplexity, curiosity and wonder. They experience the pleasure of agreement, the frustration of disagreement. They meet confusion, struggle and disenchantment. They learn to manage excitement, disappointment and embarrassment. All of these emotions feature in the mental states that are characteristic of the process of philosophical enquiry. Their emotions are often visible in the children's facial expressions and physical postures: a furrowed brow, a serious look, a mouth open, the eyes absent, brimming with tears or alight with the spark of recognition or a whole body bursting to speak.

Children discuss things that really matter to them. They gain direct experience of the difference that the dialogue can make to their being in the world. Some exchanges of ideas provoke laughter and some produce tears of grief. Sometimes the dialogue is a playful adventure. 'How do we know whether aliens exist or not?' On other occasions the dialogue may touch directly on matters of great personal importance. 'Can we talk to people after they die?'

### Personal experience

In seeking to find answers to philosophical questions that arise from stories, poems or other starting points, children make connections and draw comparisons with examples from other stories, programmes they have seen on television, or ideas that have been reported in books or elsewhere. These comparisons help shed light on the matter under discussion. Children make extensive use of things that have happened in their own lives. They do so for a number of reasons. Young children have not generally acquired large quantities of public knowledge about the world. Their personal knowledge is direct and familiar. They can speak with confidence and self-assurance about their experience, their world and their life.

It is also peculiar to them, so they have a sense of expertise and are offering original cases for consideration. Anna's attempt to understand why her teddy is not in the place where she left it, and Jack's suggestion that punching someone would finally put a stop to the harassment suffered by his family, are just two examples already described in earlier chapters. The unique detail of these particular examples is a matter of great importance. Children will often spend a long time elaborating on such instances and pointing out all the circumstances that make up the case they are bringing.

Time must be made for listening to the details if they are to be instructive. Children also show attention to detail when they offer hypothetical examples. In a classroom, these accounts provide insight into the complexities of individual thinking. They show how children manage dilemmas arising from conflicting values between home and school and between the adults in their lives.

## Including children's personal experiences in philosophical dialogue

Children's personal experiences may well become the focus of the enquiry itself. They may be part of a meta-dialogue. They may become both. It is often the case that when children relate a theme in a story to something that has been significant in their own lives the enquiry seems both precarious and powerful. It creates rather different teaching opportunities from when the enquiry is more playful or fanciful.

In the story *The Island of the Skog* a group of mice leave their home because of persistent harassment by a cat. They take a model ship and supplies and they sail away in search of a new and safer home. On the way they read that the island which they intend to colonise is inhabited by a skog. When they arrive near the island they bombard it with cannon balls. When they land they see huge footprints. They set traps for the skog. Soon they discover that the skog is a tiny creature who, in his fear of the newcomers, has dressed himself up as a monster. They make peace and agree to live in harmony together.

After watching a video of the story, a group of children were asked whether anything had happened in the story that reminded them of their own experience or what they knew of the world. They identified parallels between the behaviour of the cat towards the mice and teasing or bullying. Linda came out with the phrase 'jumping to conclusions'. She said that adults sometimes jump to conclusions about children's behaviour. Others identified themes such as flight from danger, invasion, and war.

Becky said she was interested in bullying because it reminded her of incidents of racist bullying that she had seen on television. The children then put their questions about bullying (Box 3). One person's idea triggers other examples. This is illustrated in the structural similarity of successive questions. The children wanted to begin by exploring racist bullying. They speculated about possible reasons for it. They suggested that such bullying might occur because the perpetrators were jealous, bored, showing off to impress others, thought it was cool or fun, because they thought they were better than others, or in order to avoid being bullied themselves.

*Box 3*  Children's questions about bullying

'Why do people sometimes pick on one family?'
'Why do some people pick on other people that aren't the same as them?'
'Why do bullies pick on people that haven't picked on them?'
'Why do bullies pick on new children at school?'
'Why do people pick on people who have been injured and have scars?'
'Why do bullies pick on old people?'
'Why do people pick on people they don't even know?'

The children seemed not to focus particularly on racism in their contributions other than to condemn it unanimously as unfair and wrong. There was some discussion about whether everyone is the same and whether differences should matter. One reason why it was hard to explore racism as a particular phenomenon with this group was that they had little or no direct experience upon which to draw. They lived in a rural setting where there were very few members of ethnic minority groups and where racism was hidden or found no immediate target. The children were familiar, however, with other types of bullying, and as soon as these experiences were introduced the discussion was able to make further progress.

Karen helped us to get started on a new tack. 'I think that people bully for popularity . . . I've got bullied a couple of times because I had a row with one of my friends, and 'cos she was more popular than me they all stuck up for her and I got bullied 'cos nobody liked me.'

A change of emotional climate was evident in the room as soon as this personal disclosure was made. In terms of the meta-dialogue referred to earlier, it was important to acknowledge that there could be some risk in exploring this example. It might bring back all kinds of strong feelings associated with the incident. It was an opportunity to consider how talking about experiences of people in the group might need to be managed in a different way to those from stories or the television. The disclosure made it important to be more watchful.

How possible is it to learn from such a highly charged personal experience in the public domain? In such circumstances the teacher or adult can make a huge difference to the level of risk involved in exploring a difficult issue. Respect for individual feelings is crucial and it is easy to misjudge. Acute observation, sensitivity and regular checking with the people in question are vital. Asking Karen whether it was okay to pursue her example gives her control and signals to the rest of the group that there is an issue of control. Making constructive use of the example is an opportunity for both psychological and philosophical insight.

## What is power?

Karen's story triggered lots of other accounts from children about being bullied at school. One child talked of Year Sixes (the class with the oldest children in primary school) bullying younger children. Another spoke of a group of older children harassing her whenever she went to the shop near her house. Between them the children found that they did have experience of extortion, name calling, being ridiculed for being different or unable to do something others could do, racist and sexist harassment, and bullying of newcomers.

An understanding of the dynamics of power began to emerge as the contexts of these familiar experiences were explored. The children noted the way people quickly take sides in such circumstances, often joining the more powerful. They observed that people often join in a group that is singling out an individual. We began to ask ourselves whether bullying is something of which we are all capable, given the right circumstances, or whether it is only certain individuals who bully? We began to think about how we were defining bullying. What could these experiences tell us about the nature of power, about human behaviour and personality?

How does bullying begin? Stephen, an eight-year-old and a relative newcomer to the class, offered us a graphic example.

> I got bullied at my last school. There were about five or six of them and they all chose to bully 'cos they wanted to make fun and they

> didn't let me play and I had no one to play with. They had things
> they didn't want to worry about and I did and when I had raisins
> they said they were rabbit droppings.

The last detail, as one might expect, provoked giggles from some
quarters. We were far removed from the feelings of the isolated and
worried boy in the dining hall that Stephen was describing. As Stephen
continued, more children looked at each other and joined in the
laughter. Who would want to mistake droppings for raisins? (My own
son once did, as a toddler, to the family's disgust and amusement.)
Stephen looked rather startled by the laughter. The class were asked
to think about whether laughing at someone who was describing being
bullied could also be construed as bullying. Was it possible that something that we might find funny in some contexts may be serious in
another? We needed to think carefully about our reactions. Stephen was
asked whether he wanted to continue. He wanted to tell us more.

> Even in this school some people say my dad is dead and they laugh.
> I know you thought it was fun, but I have got a dad now and I've
> got a step-brother which I have had for two years. I hope you never
> bully me again or say that my dad is dead and make fun of it.

Once again the mood of the group changed. In a very straightforward
and serious way, Neil, one of the children who had laughed the most,
expressed what the group as a whole had realised. It was suitably
understated.

> I think I agree with Stephen. It wouldn't be very nice if somebody
> said he was eating rabbit droppings, 'cos if you were eating and
> somebody said it to you, it wouldn't be very nice.

Stephen did indeed have something he needed to worry about. Silencing
the laughter provided a platform for Stephen. He moved us with the
intensity of his appeal.

## Emotional dimensions of participation in dialogue

The above example illustrates clearly how a range of emotions will
feature in a discussion where participants are making use of personal
experience to explore a moral issue. An understanding of psycho-
dynamics can be very helpful to the teacher in such instances. But whether
or not highly charged emotional experiences are brought forward for

discussion, everyone will learn from working with the range of feelings that accompany participation in a group. As well as the feelings that are an integral part of an individual's consideration of philosophical questions and concepts, many feelings also arise in the context of listening to others.

## Interaction in the community of enquiry

Just because philosophical enquiry aims to develop reasoning and logical thinking does not mean it must ignore the education of the emotions. On the contrary, the community of enquiry provides an ideal opportunity to do just that.

Dispassionate thinking depends on our capacity to recognise the ways in which reason and passion interact. If we feel threatened when another person disagrees with what we say, how does this impinge on our capacity to consider alternative views and explanations? Our pride can stop us from admitting that we have changed our mind. Jealousy can prevent us from choosing someone's question for discussion. We behave in ways that stop some members of the group from speaking at all. Something going on in our life can make us crave attention from others, regardless of relevance.

A ten-year old boy in one group was unable to stop the tears when other children disagreed either with his point of view or with his suggestions as to how we should work. He continually struggled with the tears and the embarrassment they caused him.

In some groups there will be at least one person who is so distracted or disaffected that they show little inclination to participate, or they disrupt the discussion. The emotional ups and downs of a group, and of the individuals within it, are crucial indicators of progress and significance. We have to observe, to tolerate, to learn from and sometimes to act decisively upon them.

## Boundaries: ethical decisions for the teacher

Schools are political institutions with identified public functions. Children do not have the same rights as adults. They are afforded a degree of protection but they are very short of power. Many children carry considerable responsibility but do not enjoy the same freedom to make choices. Children are referred to as minors. When starting a group on enquiry the teacher will normally be the one to suggest starting points for questioning. As children become more accustomed to asking questions and to choosing those they wish to discuss there comes a point when there is a natural drift to questions that have arisen elsewhere, that come directly from experience. Children may well say, 'Can we ask our own questions in philosophy?' 'Can we only ask questions from stories?' 'I've got something I want to talk about in philosophy.'

It may be that the teacher chooses to invite children to suggest things that they want to discuss. An agenda led by the interests of the children is even more likely when philosophy is a voluntary activity rather than part of the official curriculum, if it takes place in a lunchtime or after-school club. In such circumstances the teacher has to be prepared to give guidance based on ethical considerations about what should and shouldn't be allowed and to be able to explain and justify those decisions to children. This also provides fertile ground for exploring rules and conventions.

### Why do people have secrets?

In the present climate, and in a care or school setting, the very mention of *secret* almost inevitably carries an association with issues of child abuse and protection. Many adults would steer clear of secrets as a subject for class discussion. This is a pity because it means that it is a subject that has become taboo and the topic of secrets is so philosophically rich.

In a discussion that began with the issue of marital conflict and break-up, Carly said she wanted to know why mums and dads sometimes have secrets. She spoke of a photo she had seen of her mum kissing a man who was not her dad. She said her mum kept it in a secret place. At the mention of this, a number of other children said their mum or dad had a secret box or drawer. The children were very eager to explore the topic. Although eager to discuss the topic of secrets myself, I suggested that it was inappropriate to do so from the examples given because we were at risk of invading the privacy of members of our families. Those people were not present to give their consent or to explain their views. I explained the notion of confidentiality to the class by giving some examples of what it meant.

### Children's rights and authority

We are left with the question of where, when and how, children may explore such questions. We were able to have a limited discussion of the notion of personal privacy as one form of secrecy. It was limited because the experiences that had prompted the question in the first place were excluded as examples to draw upon. In explaining the idea of confidentiality I gave examples of how it is possible to relate an incident without naming names. I had suggested this for future reference but the effect was simply to dampen the discussion.

A better and more fruitful option might have been to explore the question of what kinds of secrets we might discuss without breaching confidentiality in the group. As it was, the discussion proved to be a landmark in our understanding of the boundaries of discussion. We drew upon the experience to make a decision when Ben wanted to ask a question about mental illness in his family and when Susan wanted to discuss the distressing outburst of one of the children's dads in the classroom, referred to in the first chapter. Notions of propriety and distance, as well as awareness of the limitations of adults and school, had been established within the group.

Recently I met some children from a group with whom I had worked regularly over several years. The children complained that 'some of the Year Sixes are a bit moody at the moment'. Playtimes were dominated by disagreement and telling-off. One of the pupils reported that there had been a lot of fighting in the playground and a child had been seriously injured. I was asked if I would come back and do some more philosophy because they thought it would help everyone to listen to each other and to think things through.

They had recognised the power of the application of philosophy in the management of their everyday lives. Practical philosophers now advertise in commercial and industrial journals, offering philosophy as a practical means of solving business problems. The notion of what philosophy is and what it can do is shifting. We no longer need be tied to ancient stereotypes.

# 10 Working with different age groups

'Dying is a way of sharing the world,' suggests ten-year-old Louis. We can be taken aback on occasion by the poetic and logical nature of observations made by children when it comes to matters such as life, death, morality and the universe. Their observations often exceed adult expectations and offer unanticipated insight. Perhaps this ability to surprise us arises from the young person's inventiveness with language. Children can greet new experiences as novel. They often have a less habituated or rule-bound response. This is not to suggest that everything children say on such matters is either well informed or profound. Rather, it is to suggest that age is not necessarily the most significant factor when it comes to seeking meaning.

The longer we live the more examples we can weigh up. But it may be that we are also weighed down with our prejudices, inhibitions and the conditioning of our particular culture. We regularly contradict the claim that one learns from experience. It is not how much experience we have, but what we make of it, that matters when we search for answers to philosophical questions.

In schools, adults tend to be fairly age and stage conscious. Learning goals are often identified separately for each year group. In most classrooms, children spend the majority of their time with one adult and a large number of peers born within the same twelve-month period. There is increasing emphasis on benchmarking by age, with more to learn and higher standards to reach. Teachers are told to find new ways of meeting demands for much higher levels of basic skills. They are expected to find new solutions for tackling underachievement. One result is much greater emphasis on assessment and target setting. But is it desirable to organise children into single age groups for all areas of learning?

## Thinking with the very young

Adults' views of what is appropriate education for children have altered substantially over time. The attitudes expressed in different cultures vary greatly. This is very evident in young children's development as thinkers and talkers, where so much of what we perceive and what children express depends on cultural norms and expectations, as well as on the social and economic position of children within each society.

Currently there is widespread concern about the formal instruction that the very young experience in England. Educators in countries where formal schooling starts much later believe it is cruel to teach and to assess four-year-olds in the way that is now common in English schools. There is some evidence to suggest that the English system may even be counterproductive (Mills and Mills, 1998).

The early years curriculum can be dramatically different, as is shown in the New Zealand early years curriculum *Te Whariki* (www.minedu. govt.nz/curriculum). This curriculum is in four key domains: empowerment, holistic development, family and community, and relationships. It recognises the wide variations in development in the early years and puts great emphasis on individual choice, responsibility and promoting independence. A distinctive curriculum is also found in the pre-schools of the Reggio Emilia region of Italy, emphasising the individual child, his or her relationships, community and environment (Edwards *et al.*, 1998). An exhibition of children's work from the Reggio Emilia pre-schools toured Britain during 2000. The exhibition, entitled 'A Hundred Languages of Children', showed that, under certain conditions, children are able to demonstrate a greater capacity for astute observation and thinking than is generally recognised in the English school system. The conditions that appear to make this possible include offering children considerable freedom and providing scope and resources to represent ideas in a variety of ways. Children need opportunities to question, to solve problems and room to follow hunches. They should be participating in shaping and maintaining the school environment. They deserve recognition of their autonomy as individuals.

In the Reggio Emilia pre-schools, children interact with each other socially. Apart from the social benefit, this interaction has a further importance. Children's discussion and questions are the starting points for the curriculum and the children's daily work. The children have access to a wide range of adults. These adults treat the children's enquiries with respect and offer their expertise and engage in open dialogue with the children. This interaction serves as midwife. The curriculum is born alive and vital. The children's curiosity and the adults' special skills and knowledge provide its shape.

High-quality thinking and conversation can take place without sacrificing children's physical freedom and exploratory play. The evidence from Reggio Emilia is that children's 2-D and 3-D representations and their utterances can demonstrate a capacity for abstract, creative and complex thinking.

The prime concern within this Italian pre-school curriculum is to find ways of sustaining and deepening any enquiry that children initiate, by a process of intellectual, social and emotional engagement with them. And the children do spend long periods concentrating, carefully observing. They listen to adults and to each other, and they can be seen spending long periods absorbed in both solitary and collaborative practical activity.

Philosophical enquiry is an area where adults can often be surprised by the youngest children's ability to engage and sustain participation. Whether it works or not depends on expectation, learning and social habits, the skill of the mediating adult and the starting points. The picture-book approach pioneered by the Dutch philosopher and children's librarian Karin Murris is a wonderful example of such mediation. Storywise (Murris and Haynes, 2000) is a development from Murris's earlier work that provides examples of children's enquiry with a range of age groups. An additional section, the 'Web of Intriguing Ideas', offers teachers a range of philosophical themes and an introduction to the thinking of philosophers that can enrich their mediation of children's developing ideas and their facilitation of group discussion.

## Am I dreaming?

Small groups of four-, five- and six-year-olds working within a mixed infant class responding to Maurice Sendak's well known tale *Where the Wild Things Are* (1992) ask questions like 'How did Max's bedroom turn into a forest?' 'Was Max dreaming?' 'Was it Max's imagination?' 'Were the monsters real?' 'Was Max wild because he had that suit on?' 'How come his dinner was still hot when he had been away a long time?' The children draw pictures and talk together with their neighbours in pairs and threes on the floor as they explore their ideas. They move into a circle to share their questions, which the teacher has recorded for all to see.

On another occasion they read the story again. Several copies of the book are made available. Some children can read some of the text while others listen and look at the pictures. The children revisit their questions and again there is some reading and some listening. A discussion about dreaming develops. David says, 'I think we're dreaming about doing work.' Linda disagrees. 'I don't think we're dreaming, because the juniors are here.' Natalie adds, 'We're not dreaming because we didn't go to sleep first.'

This view is confirmed by Robert, who says, 'We only have dreams when we're at home in bed.' A few days later one of the five-year-olds says to the teacher, 'Maybe I'm dreaming now. Maybe we're all dreaming. Maybe everyone in the whole world is dreaming. Maybe we won't wake up.'

One of the powerful features of this approach is that adults too are drawn into the philosophical discussion. Where stories are well chosen they should appeal not only to children but to adults too. This is because they express familiar but unresolved aspects of the human condition and because they are sufficiently ambiguous and complex to invite speculation from the reader or listener. *Where the Wild Things Are* tends to evoke a strong response from everyone. Some people find it mysterious and amusing, others find it fearful. The book's themes include good and evil, anger and love, time, dreaming and imagination. After reading it, and having been invited to explore their own response, adults have asked questions like 'Why do we want to eat those we love?' 'Did Max deserve to be punished?' 'How should we express our wild side?' 'Was Max dreaming?'

## The benefits of mixed-age groups

This kind of enquiry does make it feasible to abandon concern about age-related attainment and to focus on other aspects of learning, personal and social development. It's a different kind of quest altogether and one that tends to rearrange our perceptions of cleverness or achievement. It can have an equalising effect regarding individual claims to knowledge or truth. In his explanation of the characteristics of Socratic teaching Peter Abbs (1994) explains that 'education is an activity of mind, a particular emotional and critical orientation towards experience'. Socrates' teaching method was called the elenchus. The idea is to open a space for learning through getting rid of junk that can clutter up the mind and prevent it from clear and fresh thinking. It involves both the intellect and the emotions in challenging previously held beliefs and assumptions. Abbs writes, 'teaching is an ethical activity and education is, in part, the act and art of releasing a critical–ethical process in the other, the final outcome of which cannot be known in advance.' In the community of enquiry the teacher is necessarily an authentic participant and one who needs to demonstrate the virtue of the elenchus.

There are many benefits to be gained from conducting philosophical enquiries in mixed-age groups. There's the simple element of variety and surprise, for a start. Once children have overcome any initial doubts about what they can learn from younger pupils, or worries about learning alongside older ones, the lifting of age restrictions and boundaries can prove liberating. There are the obvious gains in terms of operating in different interpersonal settings. It makes everybody think again about the whole idea of knowledge being acquired from a more knowledgeable other and in stages or steps. It presents different challenges for teachers and frees them up to see another side of their pupils.

The questions that emerge from any group are naturally inclined to reflect their interests and position. But when you compare questions that have come from various groups in response to the same story, it's immediately obvious that there are overlaps. While the questions express a group's immediate position or perspective, they often lead to the same major areas of philosophical enquiry.

## Schooling and learning

Tony Bradman's *Michael* (1990), humorously illustrated by Tony Ross, relates the story of a boy who does not fit in to school, persistently refuses to conform and gets on with his own thing in spite of being written off by his teachers. At the end of the story he flies off in a rocket that he has constructed, after extensive independent research, from recycled parts. The teachers then claim that they 'always knew he would go far'.

I have kept a record of the questions asked by three different groups of people after reading this story: a class of junior pupils, the staff of a primary school and a group of teacher trainers in Poland. The children asked themselves questions such as 'How has Michael learned to make a rocket when he hasn't listened in lessons?' 'Should children be able to learn what they want?' 'The British teachers asked, 'How did Michael know what to do?' 'Why was Michael so determined?' In Poland the teacher trainers wanted to enquire 'Is being a nonconformist dangerous or liberating?' 'What sort of education should Michael have?'

In their discussion the children (ages seven to eleven) reflect on some of the issues:

JAMES: He is not actually being naughty when he is reading about rockets, it's just he's learning about something different to what everybody else is doing. He is learning about rockets instead of learning what everyone else is learning.

KYLIE: I think I know what James's thought means. I think he means that when like Mike, whatever his name is, grows up that he might build a real rocket, as he makes all these play ones.

TAMSIN: I agree with Kylie because, just 'cos you are not interested in school and what they are learning in school it doesn't mean that out of school you can't learn about something you want to learn about.

JANE: He was naughty in a way, but he wasn't. He was naughty for not listening to what the teacher was saying and learning, but he wasn't being naughty by learning his own thing about rockets.

STACEY: I agree with Tamsin because he is learning and he isn't learning, he is not doing what the teacher wants him to do, he is doing what he wants to do, but he is still sort of learning about rockets, instead of about maths or science or whatever.

LAURA: You could hardly call him all naughty because instead of playing football and everything at playtime he learnt on his own, like he was reading instead of playing football.

KYLIE: I agree with Laura because in some ways they should be happy because he is learning, like he is learning how to read, but he is not reading the books that are in school, he is reading his own kind of thing.

In their discussions, teachers and teacher trainers also used this story and their questions as a starting point to explore their ideas about the nature and purposes of schooling and the differences between schooling and learning. What may be gained and lost by bringing pupils, teachers and teacher trainers together for such a discussion?

## So does age matter?

Employers and educational policy makers have identified the need for learners to be flexible and adaptable. Children, we are told, should be morally sophisticated. They should be problem solvers, decision makers and creative thinkers. What kind of pedagogy makes such learning possible? There appears to be a tension between the more independent learning offered by modern educational technology and other demands on school pedagogy for more face-to-face instruction from the teacher. Can we meet these conflicting demands and leave enough room for initiative and independent enquiry? Can we ever get the balance of learning and teaching styles right?

In his delightful little book *Conversation*, Theodore Zeldin (1998) comments on the narrowing effect that over-specialisation can have on the capacity to converse. He also points out that discussion, talk and conversation feature more prominently than ever in the workplace. So what effect does over-specialisation in the primary classroom have on children's ability to converse? Many people in recent years have expressed concern at what they see as children's declining powers of speaking and listening. If we follow Zeldin's argument, it is over-specialisation within the curriculum that must bear at least some of the responsibility. How is it that increased attention to language may have become one of the main causes of a loss of ability and opportunity for conversation?

Much of what is done in schools is organised on the assumption that children are at a certain 'stage' in their development. It is useful to think about our assumptions regarding particular stages in learning and to ask whether it is always helpful to work with single-age groups. Why are we so fixated on age? What are we missing by sticking so firmly to one particular way of organising learning?

## Enquiry-based learning: aspects of classroom organisation and management

- Think carefully about starting points, in terms of both resources and ways of opening a lesson.
- Avoid always sticking to the same routine: go for surprise.
- Cross subject boundaries in different areas of teaching: start a science lesson with a piece of music, a history lesson with a poem, and so on.
- Be flexible and responsive in planning and preparing teaching, consult children at the planning stages and be willing to change plans.
- Make more room for children's questions, for example at the beginning of topics and lessons, and record and display these. Refer to them in teaching and return to them in review and evaluation.
- Make sure displays reflect the progress and process of work and not just the finished product: give a sense of the evolution of ideas.
- Respect children's ownership of their work.
- Rethink boundaries of age and ability and subject matter.
- Make room for enquiries, suggestions, alternative solutions and plans initiated by children.
- Share the ownership of the classroom and include children in decision making about the organisation of space and resources.
- Make time for freewheeling and exploration.
- Make time for silence and reflection.

# 11 Holding and extending threads of thinking

How does a teacher help children to pursue a particular line of enquiry? How can the teacher let the enquiry develop according to children's interests and yet provide effective structure and discipline? The following is an account of an enquiry carried out over a period of two terms. The children who participated attended a small village school and those aged seven to eleven were grouped in one class of about twenty. The children had a session of philosophical enquiry about once a fortnight.

I told the children that I was interested in their thinking, in what was going on in their minds, when we read certain stories or poems together. In some of the early sessions of work, in exploring the nature of thinking, the children raised questions such as 'How many thoughts can you hold in your mind?' and 'What if your mind gets too full of thoughts and there's no room?' These discussions led me to suggest to the children that they draw a representation of their minds on paper. It was just a brief excursion on this occasion, but their work on minds resurfaced on many occasions. Many themes continue to emerge at different times in children's discussions, just as they do among any group of people discussing philosophy.

One of the most popular discussions in this group emerged from books in which animals play a critical part in the unfolding of the story. A dog experiences jealousy. Chickens compete for the title of princess and elephants respond to violin music. These books stimulated a wealth of questions.

'How could the king and the chickens communicate?'
'How come the elephants could dance?'
'How could the dog talk to the woman?'

All these stories feature in Karen Murris's *Teaching Philosophy with Picture Books* (1992).

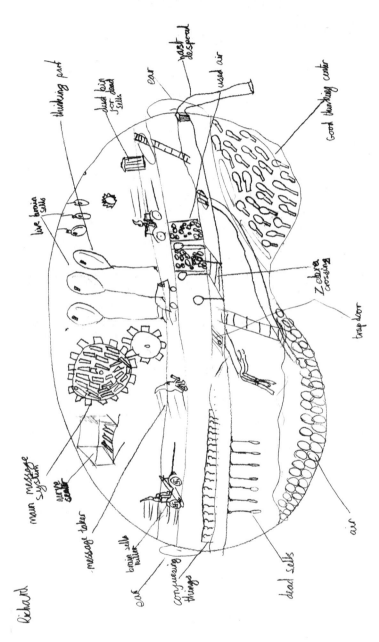

*Figure 5* Richard's brain-like diagrammatic drawing of his mind

*Figure 6* Kelly's mind picture, including a moral dimension, with a good side and a bad side

On three separate occasions, out of a range of possible questions, the children opted to pursue the question of the animals' behaviour. Each time the discussion would begin with the claim that such behaviours were uncharacteristic of animals and highly unlikely. Almost everyone present would follow with a host of examples to indicate that many animals could indeed communicate with human beings and perform like humans too. These examples were often given by the children who had originally claimed that communication was out of the question. In these enquiries firm conclusions were not generally sought or reached, and discussion would frequently continue into the playground and beyond.

At a subsequent meeting children were asked if they could see any connections between these topics. They worked in two groups to try and summarise on paper the arguments that could be put forward to suggest similarities and differences between human beings and other animals (Box 4). The mood in the two groups quickly became heated

*Box 4* Similarities and differences between animals and humans

| *Similarities* | *Differences* |
|---|---|
| Because we are like mammals | Humans are not like chickens |
| We are evolved from monkeys and they are animals | because they don't lay eggs |
| Parrots can imitate people in talking | We are not like gerbils because we don't have long tails |
| Dogs can signal | We clean our teeth with toothpaste |
| We get the same diseases as animals | We wear shoes |
| All mammals run or move fast | Animals do not make their own transport |
| All females produce babies if they have sexual intercourse | Humans look very different |
| All animals have brains, some have brains like we do | We make up hairdos |
| All animals dispose of their waste | |
| All animals have feelings | |
| Some animals wear clothes | |
| Animals use tools | |

and some children treated it as a competition. A few quarrelled about the grouping. One or two became very dominant, and one child was very angry and upset when challenged. There was an unprecedented show of strong emotion by two children in particular.

There was little time left and the children read out their lists and there was some challenge to particular points and speculation on the experience of various animals. Children were invited to give a final word around the group and Elizabeth was the last to speak. She said, 'Well, if I was a slug, I would be thinking "Ugh, this is horrible being a slug."'

## Pouncing on an idea: holding and pushing for depth

Elizabeth had articulated a thought which seemed to me on the spur of the moment to contain seeds of progress. I seized on her comment, drew it strongly to the attention of the class and informed the children that the next session we would deal with the question of the slug and what it might or might not be thinking.

At the beginning of the next meeting I read to the children the notes I had kept of their discussion.

> I've thought a lot about what happened last time. It seemed to bring out strong feelings about beliefs. That was important to do. Some people needed more time to speak – some may have been quiet, listening or even silenced by the others.
>
> (J.H. notes, 28 June 1997)

The children seemed thoughtful about this and there were some nods and comments of agreement. I told the children that it was my intention to push their thinking further, to go beyond the limits reached so far. They smiled at this and rose in their seats to the full height of anticipation. They were reminded that the only ideas under discussion would come from Elizabeth's statement. Pupils were given time for some silent, private thinking and I provided paper for notes and drawings.

## Germination of ideas

The three elements of the question began to emerge. Most of the children worked on the two ideas of 'If I was a slug' and 'This is horrible being a slug'. They expressed concern about being stood on, being slimy, being eaten by birds and eating slug pellets. Some imagined themselves as slugs. Jake said, 'I really want to stay myself.' Several children referred

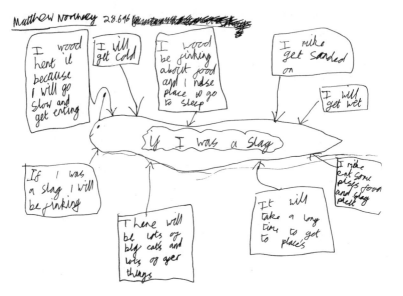

*Figure 7* If I was a slug . . .

to the idea of the slug thinking. Some represented their ideas in the form of thought bubbles on their drawings. Linda wrote, 'I think a slug thinks different, because they do not think, "Yes, chips today"'.

Robert volunteered to begin the whole-class discussion. 'I think that a slug would have to be thinking, because if he didn't have a brain or it wasn't thinking, it wouldn't be able to move or slither and it wouldn't be able to breathe or anything, so it would be sort of dead without a brain.' There were a number of other examples of what the slug would be unable to do. These ideas continued the interchangeable use of brain and thinking. Tom added, 'I agree with Robert and Katie because if you didn't have a brain you wouldn't know who you are, what you are, and everything else, because you wouldn't know anything.'

Tom tried to point out what he saw as the problem of using *brain* and *thinking* interchangeably. 'I disagree with Robert because we're not saying it doesn't have a brain. We're saying it doesn't think, and thinking and brains are two totally different things, 'cos you cannot think and still have a brain . . . well, if you don't have a brain you can't think, but if you do have a brain you don't have to think.' In the event, the children interpreted this in different ways. Some agreed that they didn't always think although they had brains in the sense of the brain being somehow inactive, switched off, or not thinking productively. Linda said that if people were like her when she was 'in a mood', they wouldn't be able to think about anything.

Some time later Robert returned directly to Tom's remark. 'I disagree with Tom because I think that if you have a brain you're thinking all the time because even when you are asleep you dream and things. And that's thinking in a way, and even when you are sitting not doing anything, you're still thinking of things.' Elizabeth added, 'I disagree with Tom and I sort of agree with Robert because everybody's got a brain, I should think ... If you didn't have a brain and you were thinking I don't know what you'd be able to think with because there would just be an empty space in your head with nothing there.'

The discussion continued with ideas about what would happen to the slug in the absence of a brain until Matthew drew on evidence from his observations of slugs seeming to demonstrate intentions. 'If slugs didn't have brains they wouldn't be able to go along anywhere, 'cos I see slugs going, heading towards something and that, walls and soil and flowers ... if they didn't have a brain they would just be going around in circles,' and Justin added, 'I agree with Matthew because every time I see a slug they are usually headed somewhere.'

In her usual humorous fashion Linda suggested that slugs must have knowledge of a kind. 'I think slugs do have brains 'cos if they didn't they wouldn't know what to eat because if you sat down and the slug was near you with your bare feet then it could eat your toes if it didn't know what to eat.' Lee suggested another aspect of slug knowledge. 'If they couldn't think or they didn't have any brains when you touch their big long eye things they go in ... so it protects them, doesn't it?' I asked Lee whether the slug must be thinking in order to react when it was touched and he replied with confidence, 'If someone was like going to be hitting us you'd think to move out of the way.'

The children were surprised to find that they had run out of time. There were spontaneous exclamations of 'That was good!' 'That was great!' 'I enjoyed that.' There had been a focus and intensity about this session, which seemed to bear the fruit of previous effort.

## Some lessons for the teacher

Susan Gardner (1996) points out that the facilitator must be a firm guide and ever vigilant, maintaining direction and forcing depth with respect to the philosophical truth towards which the enquiry points. She refers to this as progress towards the goal, which makes the enquiry worth while. Gardner talks about the tension felt by the facilitator 'being pulled between the two ideals of "truth" and "participant autonomy"'.

The tension described is evident in the experience of the facilitator of enquiry with the children mentioned in this account. There may be a tension between the teacher's understanding of a question, the direction in which she is inclined and the attention to detail which the students often bring to discussion, which may have been overlooked.

Matthew Lipman (1997: 3) argues that would-be teachers of classroom philosophy 'need to be able to distinguish essentially decidable concepts from essentially contestable concepts, if they are to understand why only the latter are truly philosophical'. Gardner suggests that 'a facilitator's own interest in the perplexity of the question may be the best guide in philosophical discussions'. Perplexity has an affective component that exists in addition to a state of cognitive uncertainty. Teachers of philosophy in primary schools may have to think about how to respond to perplexity, which they do not initially share, in order to allow discussion to proceed with authenticity and to achieve the philosophical insight which is the most significant indicator of progress.

## Providing structure and freedom in the community of enquiry

Central to the provision of structure in enquiry is the appropriate use of teacher questioning. Teachers need to become accustomed to using questions in a variety of ways:

- *Listening and clarifying.* Could you explain what you mean, could you say it in another way? Could you give an example?
- *Expanding and probing.* What are your reasons for saying that? Why do you think that is the case? How could we find that out? Are you assuming that . . .?
- *Connecting, generalising and making distinctions.* So you agree/disagree with . . .? Is that always the case? What is the difference between $x$ and $y$?
- *Speculating, exploring implications and context.* What if . . .? Is it possible that . . .? Does it change our perspective? Can we apply this to all situations?
- *Evaluating, reviewing, summarising, concluding.* Do we all understand the different viewpoints? Can anybody summarise what we have said? What have we learned?

Teachers also offer support to the development ideas by *recognising opportunities* for philosophical thinking, *making connections* between different ideas and enquiries, giving children feedback about *recurring themes* in their discussion and by demonstrating a variety of ways of *mapping ideas*.

# 12 Planning and monitoring progress in enquiry

Teachers are always concerned to ensure children are intellectually challenged, make good progress in learning and do not waste their time at school. Progression implies both a sequence or series of steps, and development in a non-linear sense. In both senses used here progression also means allowing learning to follow its course. What does this mean: 'follow its own course?' It is not a recipe for 'anything goes' but rather a concern for responsiveness to the inner dynamics of each class, both as a collective body and as a group of distinct individuals. In philosophical dialogue the interests and concerns of each community of enquiry will determine its course and the degree to which the community is able to evolve as a reflective group. Success often depends on spontaneity in the sense of seizing that which is alive in discussion. Enquiry lessons need to remain responsive to pupil interest, local conditions and events.

It is perfectly possible to plan for progression in philosophical enquiry in ways that satisfy school requirements to provide written medium and short-term plans. The planning of philosophical enquiry can link with, and be part of, a formal curriculum. Most teachers seem to link work with the formal curriculum for English, the Humanities and Personal and Social Education. In planning for encouraging collaborative enquiry in the classroom teachers will want to take children's age and experience into account. Whatever is being learned, a great deal depends on how much previous experience learners have had.

Teachers may plan for progress in a general sense in managing discussion and try to focus attention on aspects of participation in a class discussion that will help the class as a whole to do justice to the topics and questions chosen on each occasion. Such planning might look something like the example in Box 5 of plans for a junior class. These areas of interest provide the teacher with direction in planning activities for a session and in guiding the children's attention during

*Box 5* Plans for a period of half a term

---

**Discussion processes**
Making connections between questions and issues
Grouping questions under appropriate headings
Identifying different types of question

**Social and emotional learning**
Changing our minds and opinions
Working co-operatively and collaboratively in a small group
Sharing tasks out in a small group
Supporting each other

**Emotional learning and development**
Recognising personal strengths and limits of self-control
Learning to cope with challenges to one's views
Learning visualisation and relaxation techniques
Recognising the benefit of a personal boundary space

**Physical well-being**
Improving the quality of relaxation and concentration exercises
– using an object to focus attention
Keeping to personal boundaries of space to benefit self and others

---

a session. Session evaluations are also referred to these domains and to those in Box 9. These medium-term plans are addressed over a half-term period and through a sequence of lessons in which various themes are interwoven. There is also a need to choose some content such as stories, videos, or children's own questions. This content choice will be a highly personal one and will reflect the children's interests and familiarity and confidence with the process of philosophical enquiry (Box 6).

## Progression through identifying individual teachers' questions

Some teachers will choose to include a focus on their own teaching and on concerns they may have about individual children in the class. Teachers can improve this process of preparation by noting down issues and questions that they want to work on. What follows is an example

*Box 6* Choosing material to begin enquiry and dialogue prompted by stories

Look for stories, pictures, animations, poems or objects on the basis of their power to express ambiguity, to provoke puzzlement and to evoke a deep response. The material should prompt the kind of questions that cannot be quickly settled by observation or by reference to facts. There needs to be plenty of room for uncertainty and possibilities.

You may well be working with a text that fits in with a current topic. But you need to be sure that this choice does not lead you to try and influence the direction of enquiry.

Whatever you are working with, it needs to be available to everybody.

taken from a teacher with three years' experience of teaching philosophical enquiry to primary children:

How can I help two children in the class to be less distracted and disruptive and to offer their ideas?

How can I encourage greater depth in discussion without staying for too long on one issue?

How can I vary the ways we work in philosophical enquiry to avoid routinism?

How can I be more observant during our work?

How can I improve the suitability and variety of my responses to points made in discussion?

Am I catering for the youngest and the oldest children in the class?

Does it matter that one boy hardly ever speaks in the whole class setting?

Such questions help the teacher to remain alert to certain aspects of children's learning and to direct observation and action during each session. They will also focus the mind for reflection between sessions. At the end of a term's work the teacher may feel it is worth while making notes about each child in the group to add another dimension to monitoring. Another very useful evaluative tool is the recording and analysis of critical incidents (Tripp 1993). There are examples of such episodes, and the thinking that is prompted by them, in the first chapter of this book.

*Box 7* Preparation and planning

Preparing to support the children's dialogue will involve thinking about them as a group and as individuals. What will help them to listen to each other? How can you tune in to their thinking? How can you catch hold of the threads of discussion and try to push it further, without taking over? Where should attention be focused, on asking questions, on giving reasons for ideas, on following on from one another, on becoming calm and still?

Part of the preparation for the content of an enquiry is considering your own response to the material you have chosen. What do you find thought-provoking about it? What questions does it elicit in your mind? What feelings does it evoke? What responses do you anticipate from the children?

## Recording children's questions and comments

Another way to keep a record of progress is to periodically record the sorts of comments that children make during discussion. This can be done by tape-recording and transcribing or by jotting down comments made at particular stages of discussion.

The teacher has recorded all the closing comments made by children who have been discussing a video-recording of *Changes, Changes* by

*Box 8* Notes for Pat Hutchins, *Changes, Changes* (video version)

| *End-of-lesson notes* | *Child* |
| --- | --- |
| If a blind person listened to the video, I think the music was kind of miming the words so they could imagine in their heads. The music was miming for the people. | B. P. |
| Every time the music changed it's a different set of words for blind people. They'll know when the vehicles are moving, the music sounds like words. | J. W. |
| Music is saying the words for the people. | N. N. |
| The music could tell the story. Whenever something different happens, it's a different tune. | E. S. |

Pat Hutchins (1987), a story with no words which is accompanied by music in the film version. The teacher was careful to record as far as possible the children's actual words and ways of expressing their ideas. Box 8 shows a few examples from that class.

### Feeding-back to children

The discussion ended at this point. The teacher read back to the children some of the further questions that she had heard during their discussion. These are the questions that emerged as the children explored the initial questions raised in response to a story. It is not uncommon for further questions like these to conclude a series of sessions of enquiry on one particular theme. They can be parked and revisited at a later date if the teacher feels that they can usefully connect with or enrich a subsequent enquiry. There is no need for an enquiry to be resolved.

- What story can music tell us?
- What was the story – is there only one?
- Did we make words when we watched the video or did we make a story without words?
- Do blind people see pictures in their minds when they hear music?

This class sustained an enquiry over several weeks. They worked in small groups and an early sifting of questions helped to maintain the focus for the whole class. They were able to comment on their own performance as small teams. They chose a question that was philosophically rich. When they discussed their question they kept to the point, although they sometimes opened up sub-lines of enquiry. There were no premature attempts to answer the question. The work they did in their groups on their chosen questions and on the chosen subject all reveal the scope for the future development of this community of enquiry.

*Box 9* What are we looking for?

---

In speaking and listening we look for:

- Addressing one another
- Asking and answering questions
- Reference to one another's ideas
- Clear explanation
- Attentive listening.

In personal and social development we look for:

- Support for one another
- Tolerance and respect
- Building on one another's ideas
- Taking turns

In questioning and reasoning we look for:

- Open questions
- Giving reasons and asking for evidence
- Examples and counter-examples
- Exploring alternatives
- Seeking clarification
- Drawing comparisons and distinctions
- Noticing our own thinking.

---

## Predominant ideas about progression

Teachers are accustomed to planning for progression through managing the order in which material is presented to a class or through a building-blocks approach in which the level of difficulty is gradually increased. The teacher who follows a written curriculum retains the initiative for ensuring that progression takes place. In most primary schools, schemes of work are drawn up for half a term at a time. These schemes of work exist in a detailed form for all subjects in the curriculum and for each year group in the school. The aims and objectives are given and they are non-negotiable. This rigidity is evident in the language that describes the teaching of the curriculum in terms of *coverage* and *delivery*. The teacher's job is to interpret this scheme and to plan how it will be carried out week-by-week and day-by-day. The teacher adapts the implementation of a scheme of work through the short-term planning according to the children's responses.

The language of teaching as *delivery* comes from the industrial model used by central curriculum creators. It has appeared because the statutory, nationally determined curriculum derives from a vision of education as mainly preparing children for employment. Planners claim to know what employers need and have agreed to supply what they are seen to be demanding. In order to provide an employment-oriented curriculum, the central planners of the school curriculum have reduced the status of individual, personal fulfilment. The philosophical notion of education as a personally fulfilling and worthwhile pursuit has been massaged. Pupils are now expected to derive satisfaction and a sense of worth directly from achievements that are primarily focused on ensuring they develop skills that make them employable.

It is this fundamental shift to education as *product* that has cost us the arts in education, and led to a philistine curriculum couched in business language of *delivery*, *levels* and *standards*, which is increasingly being rejected as lacking in quality or humanity. It is a centralised system for the delivery of standardised schooling to children brought about through the medium of teachers as agents of the state.

Apart from the economic need to compete in the global economy through improved education and training of the country's work force, the state system has a long-standing case to answer to a substantial number of individuals who finish twelve years of schooling with little to show for it. In that sense there can be no argument with the principle of raising standards. In the debate about improving standards the importance of ensuring progression in learning has been argued strongly.

## What is progression?

What understanding do we have of this concept and what associations can be made with the term 'progression' in the present educational climate? Making sure that progression and continuity are achieved has led to an increase in the time teachers spend planning, timetabling, assessing and keeping records. Teachers have become adept at clock watching and objective chasing. Competition, challenge, comprehensive documentation and the drive forward are seen to be some of the hallmarks of the successful school.

What's the problem with this model and this vision of education? The prescribed approach to planning and managing the curriculum has affected the day-to-day and moment-by-moment experience of teaching children, the relationship between teacher and learner and the type of interaction that takes place in the classroom. Some of this change has been for the good but it has also led to difficulty. Two of the most highly prized skills of business and commerce are *problem solving* and *creative working in groups*. These two skills are bound to be among the earliest casualties of a recipe-driven curriculum that is centralised and prescriptive.

A prescriptive curriculum requires that teachers dictate pace, direction, coverage and product. This requires that children follow instructions. When something happens that has not been planned for, it is seen as a deviation that puts the delivery of desired outcomes for a lesson at risk. The result is over-reliance on the teacher. And this is despite the recognition by many people, in business and elsewhere, that children must learn to become adaptable lifelong learners who can manage a very uncertain future.

Key skills to be learned are in fact, a sense of what is moral and right, a realistic belief in oneself, adaptability in a changing labour market, openness to innovation and change, the ability to manage complexity, the willingness and confidence to live alongside others with different cultures, habits and beliefs. Where is this training evident in the formal curriculum that schools are required to follow?

A further problem produced by the *delivery* conception of curriculum is the effect on teaching behaviour. Pressure to stick rigidly to a scheme of work, to lesson plans and their specific objectives, now dominates the minds of teachers. The inspection process has become a method of measuring deviance, and deviance is harshly punished. The result is that belief in teaching as a vocation, and a service, becomes fragile. Teaching may well become perfunctory, superficial, lacking fluidity and creativity. No longer seen as a vocation, it is no longer a service to children and their parents.

All this is not an argument for abandoning planning, or giving up the production of schemes of work. It is a criticism of the obsessive and prescriptive culture that has led to over-planning, the narrowing of the exercise of choice for teacher and children and to the planning of *knowledge delivery* at the expense of preparation for critical thinking.

The over-detailed and over-prescribed curriculum with its corresponding approach to planning, driven mainly by the need to ensure that everything listed is *covered*, has led to a situation in which teachers rarely feel able to allow learning to take off in unpredictable or unexpected directions. Teachers are expected to retain most of the control and initiative and, in such cases, there is indeed an answer in the teacher's head at which the pupils must, one way or another, arrive.

In classes where children's contributions are strongly encouraged and where they are invited to make personal responses to a stimulus, teachers still feel obliged to keep making the connections back with the original objectives in the lesson plan. Even if more than one pathway is allowed, the finishing point must be the same. These pressures and constraints have had a profound effect on the experience of teaching and learning. They limit the opportunities to develop children's thinking and their independence or initiative. Creative teaching has survived where teachers are confident and well led or sufficiently gifted to mediate the negative effects of constant change and interference. On the whole, there has been too much convergence on a single business and employment-oriented curriculum, with a consequent diminution in creativity and originality. A curriculum for citizenship has not been seen as sufficiently important to be incorporated into the primary school curriculum. This is of course an advantage because a citizenship curriculum with attainment levels and end of key stage objectives is anathema to a liberal, democratic society. Philosophical enquiry offers an important opportunity for teachers.

- It offers a method of teaching that undoes some of the damage caused by a prescriptive, objectives-led curriculum.
- It provides a vehicle for exploring many of the issues that are synonymous with being a participating citizen of a democracy.
- It helps teachers and children to find humane ways of assessing individual contributions and recognising personal development.

# Part IV

# The benefits of philosophical enquiry and dialogue

Chapter 13 suggests that there are considerable opportunities for teachers to develop their professional knowledge and skills through the practice of facilitating open-ended dialogue in the classroom.

- How can teachers cultivate presence and attention in classroom discussion?
- What's involved in preparing for open-ended enquiry?

Chapter 14 explains why teaching for enquiry is a good way of addressing those elements of the national curriculum in England that refer to thinking skills, communication skills, inclusion, personal and social education and citizenship. It suggests ways that philosophy can be incorporated into the timetable.

- What contribution does philosophy make to the curriculum as a whole?
- How can it be included in the timetable?

Chapter 15 draws on the opinions of children, teachers and of research and inspection reports to suggest that there are significant benefits for learners who are given regular opportunities to take part in philosophical enquiry.

- How will children benefit from philosophical enquiry?

# 13 Developing teaching skills through philosophy

Children who have taken part regularly in philosophical enquiry have argued that it is good for teachers too, quite simply because it provides the opportunity for teachers to listen to children's opinions and for children to raise the issues and questions that concern and interest them. As these two nine-year-old girls explain:

> I think that teachers should teach the pupils [philosophy] because, um, it doesn't just help the children, it helps them as well because they can understand how they feel and why they feel like that.

> I think it's a good idea to introduce philosophy to schools because it's a good subject and it helps children to think and so it's good for teachers as well.

In her research report on thinking skills in schools Carol McGuiness (1999) suggests: 'Increasingly it is recognised that developing thinking skills has implications not only for pupils' thinking but for teacher development and teacher thinking as well as for the ethos of schools as learning communities.'

Earlier chapters have hinted at the kinds of qualities that are required by adults who seek to promote children's abilities as thinkers. Open-ended enquiry makes different demands on the skills of the teacher from when she or he is able to plan for specific knowledge outcomes. Success will often depend on being able to respond in the moment to opportunities that arise and on the teacher's being comfortable with the unknown and unpredictable. So what kind of teacher qualities and skills are we talking about? My own practice with children in schools and with fellow teachers suggests that development is likely in two major areas of practice. These are presence and preparation.

## Teacher presence

The apprentice teacher often envies the ability of an experienced teacher to gain and hold effortlessly the attention of children in a classroom. Such a presence is very difficult to explain. It is also difficult for the novice to imitate. Some teachers seem to have more presence than others. Presence in the classroom is not the power of exceptional charisma. It is not simply the ability to perform or entertain, nor should it rely on intimidating children. Presence in the classroom is a manner of being. It often appears to be both deliberate and yet natural. In the classroom of a teacher with presence, children are volunteers rather than captives.

What metaphors are useful for exploring presence? Could it be that there are ingredients that can be added and mixed to the personality and the pysche? There is something in the body language, in the voice, in the attention to detail, in the hope and expectation that get communicated to the pupils. There is also a sense of intention and commitment to the task in hand. There is not only clarity and focus but also fluidity in the interactions.

Teachers who have presence attend (perhaps unconsciously) both to cognition and to affect. They can hold the class strongly enough to provide intellectual structure, firmly enough to nurture emotional confidence, yet lightly enough to allow personal freedom, choice, intellectual independence, movement and growth. Presence is not egocentric and must stop short of domination, however entertaining, that leaves no room for the thinking of pupils, especially the less self-assured.

Teachers who have this presence know learners at all three levels. There is cognitive, affective and psychic understanding of the children's needs. Presence is often developed from the experience of frequent teaching of the same group. Presence can also arise through an innate or acquired ability to recognise the particularity and uniqueness of groups and individuals. Teachers with presence also recognise what is original and special in each teaching occasion, even when the teaching requires the revisiting of familiar ground.

## Attention to the here and now

This is the second major quality found in teacher presence. Attention is the quality of alertness given to the unfolding of each lesson. Attention is paid to the children at all of the three levels described earlier. The teacher who cultivates presence also pays attention to the nature of children's particular responses to the matter in hand. The result of attending is the ability to be informed and sensitised as to mood, to timing, to new insights, to connections with other areas of learning and to the children and to one's own changing thoughts and feelings.

Attention can be both focused or unfocused. Sometimes presence necessitates attention to the most minute of detail. At other times, attention needs to be everywhere so as to open the teacher's awareness to all that is happening in the room and between all the individuals. Attention enables the teacher to observe children acutely, to comprehend what children say. Teachers can take children's responses as fuel for further teaching activity and as signposts to guide the direction of travel.

A teacher with presence also maintains genuine dialogue. Children recognise this and greatly value the experience. The consequence of genuine dialogue is the realisation that one is valued for what one does, thinks and says. One result of genuine dialogue is the maintenance of *rapport* that the teacher with presence establishes with children.

Intuition comes into play. The unexpected often happens. The teacher and the pupils are secure enough to invent the lesson between them. The lesson plan is a starting point, a springboard, a guide, rather than a recipe.

This aspect of presence is a boundary phenomenon. It belongs to the *potential space* that the teacher establishes with the children's consent and within which the teacher and the children explore the possibilities that each lesson offers. This aspect of presence *is* the interaction between pupils and teacher. It is essentially dynamic. As the teacher develops these aspects of presence so too do the pupils. They begin to work in the same way as the teacher. With growth in the children's quality of attention comes growth in their aptitude for learning.

## Preparation for teaching – preparedness to teach

In most manuals about teaching the word 'preparation' usually refers to the process of setting up the classroom, arranging furniture and seating plans, organising resources on tables, sharpening pencils, making sure that there is enough of everything, checking that audio or video equipment is working, and marking places in a text to be used. This sort of organising is intended to ensure the smooth running of lessons, avoiding the waste of precious time and reducing opportunities for disruption. It is important to give time to this kind of planning and to think who best could do it. Pupils can do much of it. This benefits the teacher, who can use the time gained for teaching preparation. It also benefits the pupils, many of whom enjoy this kind of work and who gain satisfaction from seeing their effort contribute to a successful lesson.

They are taking on greater responsibility for their surroundings and for managing the resources they use. For example, the Highscope approach to classroom organisation (Weikart *et al.*, 1971) advises making resources routinely available to pupils thereby reducing the time a teacher spends on setting up and putting away.

Teachers who are serious about promoting enquiry-based learning will certainly want to share the ownership and control of classroom organisation and resources with pupils, right from the start of schooling. Many teachers engage in other forms of preparation, probably more important, but rarely recognised or discussed.

## Rehearsal

Novices use this extensively. Rehearsal allows a mental run through the unfolding of a lesson. It allows focusing, especially on those parts that involve direct teaching through demonstration or explanation and which require the teacher to remember a sequence of steps. The more unfamiliar the material, the more there is a tendency to rehearse as if for a performance. This rehearsal gives confidence, especially in the initial stages of teaching, where novices anticipate their active performances being the focus of children's attention. Rehearsals are often concerned with performance that involves demonstration, exposition, voice projection and explanation. Later, when these have been acquired with confidence and no longer figure as the major part of the novice's repertoire, rehearsal can be detrimental.

## Dwelling

Dwelling is the idea of staying with the detail of rich episodes of classroom interaction and trying to hold on to nuances and fragments. It refers to the mental replaying of episodes from the most interesting and most recent teaching. The teacher relives material that has arisen from teaching in order to make a new kind, or another kind, of sense of it. Dwelling aids the digestion of earlier work and enables one to act upon it (Tripp, 1993).

Dwelling allows the focusing of attention on the behaviour or responses of individuals in the class. The stimulus to dwell may result from the teacher experiencing a disturbance of some kind, either positive or negative. Dwelling will include staying with the unexpected, the noticed, the exceptional and the critical moments that arise in group learning situations (Mason, 1996). Preparing to understand the value of disturbance is part of the business of teaching. Dwelling on something noticed allows on-going preparation, the fine-tuning of responses to the cognitive, affective, social and psychological dimensions of classroom life.

## Readiness

Teaching is a very demanding activity. It requires considerable intellectual, physical and emotional stamina. It involves the application of sustained focus and attention. Teachers find their own ways of being *ready for teaching* and it is very useful to ensure that one is increasingly open to one's unconscious as well as one's deliberate moves. These can include following a particular dress code, adopting a role and using language in a teacherly way. Readiness includes the capacity to compartmentalise one's life so that external concerns do not intrude during teaching. It can involve the use of mental and physical exercises to increase concentration and energy.

Readiness is based on familiarity with, and use of, strategies that help an individual teacher to prepare for the deployment of energy, creativity and attention in the classroom. It is a kind of preparation of the self, and teachers recognise only too well those times when their own lack of readiness causes difficulties in children's learning.

## Freewheeling

Many teachers make use of *freewheeling* time, when some of the best ideas surface and problems are solved. These times are periods when there is no deliberate attempt to think but solutions nevertheless emerge. Guy Claxton (1997) refers to this as accessing the intelligent unconscious. For many people these creative periods occur in the moments of surfacing from sleep. Writers, among others, recommend keeping a notepad and pen at the side of the bed to make more use of this time. Some people also find that experiences like lying in the bath, swimming, walking the dog, driving or ironing allow freewheeling to occur.

## Hooks and bridges

These are the endless, highly original ways of starting lessons, or pushing children's thinking a little bit further on. Teachers become adept at making connections between one thing and another and using these connections to enhance their teaching and their children's learning. Hooks and bridges are the tools that teachers use to gain, hold and develop the attention of the whole class and individuals. Ideas for hooks often surface in a teacher's mind during freewheeling periods of thinking outside the classroom. Bridges are very often made in the moment. If a teacher is finely tuned to the unfolding lesson then connections and bridges to previously unanticipated possibilities emerge, moment by moment. They are effective devices because they thrive on the emotional as well as the intellectual currents in the learning process.

Kieran Egan (1988) suggests that the objectives–content–methods–evaluation model can lead to mechanistic approaches to planning for teaching. Egan argues that teaching should make better use of children's and teachers' imaginations and adopt approaches in which meaning and engagement are brought to the fore. This involves identifying the aspects of a topic that are most important, in the full sense of the word, to children. It gives a story-like rhythm to teaching and learning.

### Active listening

A teacher learns to make judgements in the moment about how to respond to the unfolding lesson. This ability is acquired along with familiarity with the matter in hand, sensitivity to one's own state and to the general condition and mood of the class. In philosophical enquiry such judgements must be informed by a desire to allow the children's thinking to unravel and to leap. Creative listening removes the need for a bombardment of teacher questioning and imposed solutions. It avoids inappropriate and premature resolution. Active listening encourages all parties to partially suspend the proffering of their own answers and opinions, in order to hear and understand each other properly (Pinney, 1983). It is an essential ingredient of the teacher with presence in the classroom and it is a key element of attention.

These ideas represent just the beginning of an exploration into aspects of being a teacher that have emerged in my practice of working with children and adults in the ways described in this book. I certainly hope that they will be the sources of further investigation with other practitioners. It has been my experience that when it comes to thinking and talking about effective facilitation of dialogue most of the formulas for planning and managing discussion in current use are deeply flawed and limiting. A different language is required to try and address aspects of planning and teaching that have been neglected in the predominant rational curriculum framework.

# 14 Teaching thinking across the whole curriculum

Policy makers and practitioners are often required to satisfy the desire that people have to retain the traditional emphasis on a core of so-called basic skills and to expand the curriculum to include new areas of knowledge. Schools are also expected to solve social problems and to impart certain religious, social or moral values. We know that there is a difference between what is written into the curriculum and the learning experiences and achievements of pupils in a range of schools. The curriculum for schools is based on an identification of economic and social needs of our society. The education system is expected to prepare young people to work and to live, to contribute to and to participate in society.

We can acknowledge the political nature of conflicting interests in the curriculum. We can also argue about the overall balance of what is taught and how individual needs should be balanced with the demands of employers. But there seems to be little disagreement about what the major social and economic trends are. Any system of education somehow needs to take these into account. So what are the wider developments that the current curriculum, in Britain at least, claims to be seeking to address?

It is evident that communications technology is increasingly permeating our lives and it is hard to imagine such a trend being reversed. It influences language, literacy and learning as well as employment, services, domestic life and leisure activity. Employment patterns have changed dramatically over the last twenty-five years and will continue to do so. There are no jobs for life. The nature of the economy has shifted. It is expected that people will change jobs more often, that retraining will be common and that the boundaries between work, home life and leisure will continue to evolve. Employers put a higher premium on flexibility, on problem solving, communication and information processing skills. The abilities to work both independently and as part of a team are expected in the workplace.

In the social arena, the responsibilities and rights of individuals seem to become increasingly complex – although this is perhaps an argument that is advanced in every age. We have to make moral decisions about matters of health, reproduction, the care of the elderly and the dying, the environment. Patterns of social and family life require individuals to be able to adapt to separation, moving and change.

The growth and proliferation of information have an impact on the very idea of knowledge. Knowledge becomes increasingly transient and replaceable, more questionable and more widely on tap, at least to those with resources to access it. The roles and knowledge status of both teacher and student must change dramatically. At the same time, we need to make selections and judgements about all that we perceive. One can almost hear the creaking as schools, many functioning in buildings constructed for a very different era, try to modernise. Those buildings were designed for modes of teaching that often seem to contradict the forms of knowledge that we now seek to create and the styles of learning that they imply. The idea of school buildings to house learning is superseded in many ways by the existence of the information highways that abound.

## Aims and purposes of the National Curriculum

When the National Curriculum in England was revised for the year 2000 it contained a statement of its two major aims. The first is that

> the curriculum should build on pupils' strengths, interests and experiences . . . and promote an enquiring mind and a capacity to think rationally . . . the curriculum should enable pupils to think creatively and critically, to solve problems and to make a difference for the better.
>
> (Page 11)

The second major aim is concerned with spiritual, moral, social and cultural development and about preparation for responsibilities and experiences of adult life. Pupils are to be taught ways of distinguishing between right and wrong and about a range of beliefs. The document argues:

> the school curriculum should pass on enduring values, develop pupils' integrity and autonomy and help them to be responsible

and caring citizens capable of contributing to the development of a just society . . . promote equal opportunity and enable pupils to challenge discrimination and stereotyping.

(Page 11)

The National Curriculum argues that personal and social development, creative and critical thinking, self-confidence and the ability to collaborate with others are crucial to students' educational success and to their all-round achievement.

According to the revised National Curriculum, pupils' spiritual development includes the growth of a sense of self and entails the capacity to make responsible moral decisions. As part of their social development, pupils are expected to participate in and to make an active contribution to the democratic process in their community. Curiosity about differences between people is seen as a feature of cultural development.

The National Curriculum statement explains how it is underpinned by a view of learning across the whole curriculum. It includes guidance on developing pupils' sense of self, on cross-curricular knowledge and skills. It stresses the importance of teaching for meta-cognition and of language for learning. It includes suggestions for strategies to ensure that all pupils are included in learning.

## Philosophy with children and cross-curricular knowledge and skills

When we consider the programmes of study for different subjects in the curriculum, it becomes evident how a variety of enquiry skills are needed. Even if we cannot go along with the idea of a toolkit of transferable learning skills, the terminology used conjures up a picture of an independent and capable learner, actively engaged with investigation, with planning and appraisal, able to collaborate with others.

Let's just briefly consider examples from particular areas of the curriculum. The new framework for teaching numeracy puts increased emphasis on the application of mathematical knowledge. This entails developing pupils' ability to reason, to explain their thinking and describe their mental strategies for solving problems. Science requires the ability to hypothesise, to follow a process systematically. In history, pupils are expected to be able to examine historical evidence and to weigh up change and its consequences. In geography, students learn to assess the impact of human activity on the environment. Religious education requires students to compare different beliefs, and in design and technology students make judgements about effectiveness and quality of design and implementation. And so it goes on. The emphasis is clearly on questioning, planning, investigation, problem solving, evaluation, discussion, reasoning and enquiry.

How does philosophy with children fit in to the teaching of some of these cross-curricular skills?

- *Communication.* The medium of philosophy with children is primarily oral and children learn to use language by speaking their minds, exploring meaning and nuance, and acquiring a specific terminology for reasoning and for taking part in dialogue. They become able to listen very effectively. Through collective discussion, children learn to understand and to respond to others. Through the use of a wide range of texts for enquiry, they learn to reflect critically. The structure of enquiry supports the construction of logical argument that in turn supports discursive writing. Children develop confidence in expressing ideas and opinions and explaining them to others.

- *Working with others.* In philosophical enquiry, children contribute to small-group and whole-class discussion, learning to appreciate the experience of others and to consider different perspectives. Children are faced directly with issues of power and authority regarding knowledge. They are given time to express their own opinions and to bring their experience to bear in acquiring insights and making judgements. They get involved in tackling the problems of democratic discussion and managing differences of opinion, conflicting beliefs, strong feelings and controversial issues.

- *Improving own learning and performance.* Evaluation of the process and content of an enquiry is an integral part of philosophy with children and time is given over to it. This is part and parcel of developing both the *language of learning* and *meta-cognition*. Philosophy quite naturally addresses all kinds of questions that deal directly with problems of mind, thought, knowing, imagination, dreaming, consciousness and interaction between minds.

- *Problem solving.* The practice of philosophy not only teaches ways of approaching problems but also generates and creates new questions and problems to try and solve or unpick. In particular, children are helped to identify the nature of a problem through detailed definition, through clarifying concepts and through being able to compare and distinguish particular cases and specifying its contextual features.

- *Information processing.* In philosophy children have lots of opportunities to engage in sorting, classifying, sequencing and comparing and contrasting questions, ideas, examples, concepts. In particular, they learn ways of organising and mapping ideas and presenting information, making use of a variety of conceptual tools and forms of representation.

- *Thinking skills.* Philosophy probably wants to question the whole notion of thinking skills, let alone the separation of strands such as information processing and reasoning.

But, for want of a better way of describing these features of thinking, Western philosophy has an established reputation for developing powers of enquiry, critical thinking and reasoning and certain kinds of creative thinking. Enquiry goes beyond information to seek explanation. In philosophical enquiry children learn to pose and define problems, to question concepts and values. They get involved in analysing and assessing evidence, questioning assumptions, distinguishing between true and false, between fact and opinion. The community of enquiry provides a structure in which hypotheses can be tried out. It makes room for divergent thinking and alternative interpretations or solutions.

## Inclusion of all children

The revised National Curriculum shows particular determination to ensure that all pupils are provided with opportunities to succeed in their education. Experience in philosophy with children seems to suggest that it can have a very positive impact on the achievement of all pupils. Some evidence of this is put forward in Chapter 15.

Gifted children welcome the opportunity to use their powers of imagination, abstraction and logic and often learn to work more happily with others. Children with behavioural and specific learning difficulties benefit from the collaboration and oral work in philosophical enquiry. Children who struggle with reading and writing are able to succeed and all views are respected. Topics of discussion are wide-ranging. Children are able to develop a *sense of self* and make a contribution with confidence because of the secure atmosphere in which ideas can be tried out and because changing one's mind is an expected part of the process.

## How can philosophy be planned into the curriculum?

Philosophical enquiry can be used to enhance many areas of the curriculum. It is most likely to be appropriate in the context of subjects like English, PSHE and the Humanities. However, teachers who have used this approach on a regular basis notice that children are increasingly inclined to bring this way of thinking to other areas of learning, such as science and mathematics, as well as using it to solve problems that arise in the playground. It is an approach that allows children to develop as independent thinkers and researchers.

### Personal, social and health education and citizenship

The framework for PSHE and citizenship aims to develop informed, active, confident citizens that reflect on their experiences and tackle a wide range of social personal and political issues as part of their growing up, learning to understand and respect diversity and differences as well as our common humanity.

Philosophy with children is well placed to address the requirements that are laid down in the guidelines for the younger age group in school (five- to seven-year-olds). These include, among other things, sharing opinions and explaining views, taking part in discussion with the whole class, listening to other people, recognising choices and considering the moral and social dilemmas that they come across in everyday life. Older children in the primary school (eight- to eleven-year-olds) are expected, among other things, to talk and write about their opinions and explain their views. They should learn to understand how different rules are needed in different situations, to reflect on spiritual, moral and social issues, to participate in the decision-making process and to consider moral and social dilemmas.

### Philosophical dialogue promotes speaking and listening skills

The community of enquiry provides space and time for children to put forward their own ideas and questions within a sensitively structured setting. Expressing doubt and uncertainty, trying out theories, agreeing and disagreeing, changing your mind, are all normal parts of the process of pursuing new insight or better judgement. Children's listening develops as they come to recognise the way everyone sheds light in a different way on an enquiry.

This is a tried and tested approach that has been shown to give participants greater confidence, including the more reticent. Children particularly welcome the opportunity to explore ideas without the pressure or obstacle of writing.

## Enhancing the teaching of literacy

Where enquiry-based communities have been sustained in classrooms over a period of time, children's reading skills have been shown to improve. Teachers report that children's confidence as readers grows as they are encouraged to deconstruct and interrogate texts at a deep level. This process of enquiry allows children to grasp meaning and significance both as individuals and as classroom communities. Children start to make connections between the themes that emerge from a variety of texts, so their understanding of 'story' as a universal human form is kindled and nurtured. Children develop a sense of their power as readers and their right to question and challenge as well as to celebrate the printed word. The use of animated video as well as text promotes wider media literacy, encouraging children to become discriminating and questioning viewers as well as readers. The attention that is given to the illustrations in books extends their visual literacy in other directions.

## Including philosophical enquiry in the programme for literacy

In many schools, teachers give one of their dedicated literacy sessions over to enquiry and dialogue around a chosen text. The contemplative and learner-led approach makes a good counterbalance to the rapid pace and highly focused teaching that goes on in the skills-based section of the literacy hour.

At text level, enquiry improves children's comprehension of fiction texts and develops thinking skills that they can also bring to their reading of non-fiction. It provides opportunities for the development of the skills of prediction, making inferences and deductions. Through deep interrogation, discussion and reflection, children learn to recognise aspects of an author's style, in terms of ideas and in terms of personal ways of manipulating language. The encouragement to use precise definition and to reason and present clear argument helps prepare children to write discursively. In terms of the teaching of grammar, close reference to the text during a session of philosophical enquiry heightens children's ability to compare various forms, standard and non-standard, that writers use to achieve particular effects. At word level, children become very interested in the precise and multiple meanings of words and in authors' choice of vocabulary.

During enquiry the teacher is able to offer the children suggestions about ways of organising and recording ideas. These may include brainstorming, concept maps and webs, lists of fors and againsts, etc. These enable the teacher to show children how writing can be used to organise ideas, to plan and to clarify thinking, or to record ideas for future use. Children can share in this process.

## Philosophy with children at the Foundation Stage

Guidance published by the Department for Education and Employment (DfEE and QAA, 2000) identifies the Foundation Stage as from age three to the end of the Reception year in primary school. It recognises the distinct educational needs of children in this age group. The early curriculum is based on fostering children's personal, social and emotional well-being, positive disposition towards learning, social skills, attention skills and persistence.

The Foundation Stage guidance clearly lays down some key principles for good educational practice with children, working closely with parents, throughout this phase. Many of the principles are explicitly addressed through the kind of interaction that is part of the community of enquiry process described in Chapter 3. These principles stress the importance of a relevant curriculum, one that includes all children and builds on what children already know and can do. It emphasises that there should be space and time for children to be initiators and that adults must be able to respond appropriately and offer rich and stimulating experiences.

Philosophy with children is based on a fundamental recognition of *all* children's ability to participate in and contribute to the exploration of ideas and beliefs and the making of meaning. It is based on respect for children of all ages.

This Foundation Stage of the curriculum is based on six areas of learning and establishes goals to define expectations that most children should reach by the end of this stage. Philosophy with children can address learning in the areas of:

- *Language and communication* through planned opportunities to question, to talk and to listen.
- *Reading and writing* through carefully structured sharing of good quality stories, texts and animations.
- *Mathematics* through the exploration of mathematical language and questions, arising from stories and through the encouragement of logical thinking.
- *Knowledge and understanding of the world* through pursuing all kinds of questions and discussion that arise in the context of responding to picture books and animations.

- *Creative development* through expression of the imagination in response to questions and through dreaming of solutions to problems.

Practitioners of philosophy with children have used picture books and video animations to stimulate philosophical discussion with very young children. They are quite capable of participating in deep thinking, dialogue and enquiry of this kind. The process is easily adapted to accommodate the needs of different groups. Practitioners can create supportive conditions for learners that they know well. These will include sensitivity to age and experience; openness, patience and flexibility; the provision of rich and stimulating starting points for thinking; space and time for children to question, initiate shape or represent enquiry and a profound interest in children's ideas and feelings.

# 15 What difference can philosophy make to children's learning?

This chapter sets out to summarise the reasons for making time and space for open-ended dialogue in school. How do we know if it is worth while? What are the claims made for doing philosophy in the classroom? There is some evidence of assessable outcomes included here for readers' consideration. However, I want to suggest that judgements about whether or not philosophical enquiry is valuable are more likely to be made on the basis of beliefs about the balance of experiences that schooling and education should provide for children.

## The opinions of some children

It seems fitting to begin with some of the observations that children have made about their participation in philosophical enquiry. Teachers' judgements about including an activity in the timetable have to be made in the context of current curriculum aims and school priorities. Children in school are often very realistic about what is important and, at the same time, their perspectives can help us to look at things in another light.

One of the strongest points to emerge in reviews carried out with children is the emphasis they put on having an opportunity to speak, to have their point of view taken seriously and to have their experiences counted. Earlier in this book I have referred to children's comments on the significance of speaking without being laughed at, and we have shown how they speak of applying the 'rules of philosophy' elsewhere in their lives. This is remarkable, since achieving transferability of learning from the classroom into other contexts is a taxing problem for teachers. Perhaps the pertinence that is given to children's own questions and experiences in pursuing this type of enquiry is a feature that facilitates transfer and application. Many children value the chance to speak without the pressure to record on paper. Regular participation in this type of dialogue seems to build self-confidence.

Children stress the advantages of talking together in a number of ways. They describe the sense of feeling cared for, and not being alone, when others listen to them. They speak of the pleasure of hearing a variety of opinions, pursuing ideas, constructing argument and seeking truth. One child says that what he likes is 'having all the different arguments, finding out whether things are true or not, and discussing them all together'. Another child reports, 'Everyone has got a different opinion and we are all arguing 'cos each one has a different opinion to each question'. Lisa adds, 'I like it when we argue 'cos everybody is saying different things and then they disagree with other people and then they say that it's a lie and some say it isn't.'

## What seems significant?

Children often talk about enjoying what they describe as 'not real' and, as eight-year-old Becky describes them, 'weird conversations' that are possible when the invitation to puzzle about what goes on in stories is offered. The puzzling is playful and adventurous. Children recall the details of these conversations long after they have taken place. All genres and contexts are very popular: the magical, the fantastic, the future and the distant past, dreaming and imagination, the strange and the unusual.

Are unicorns and dragons real or true? What would it be like to meet an alien? Could a body really be frozen and revived in a hundred years' time? Exploring the boundaries of reality at the edges of fiction makes for particularly rich and memorable discussion. It creates a different kind of learning space.

## Awareness of the mind at work

Another recurring theme in children's evaluations of enquiry is the frequent reference to changing one's mind. Jamie, an eleven-year-old, often reflects on this: 'Once someone has said something I haven't said and it's good then I think of changing, 'cos it might be much better than mine.' Changing one's mind is a great source of interest and a process that adults can actively demonstrate to children to reveal how we can influence and be influenced by others. One technique is to take note of opinions before and after a discussion. For example, a class of juniors was exploring a Japanese folk tale in which a lowly stonecutter is changed into a prince (McDermott, 1975). Having read the story together, the children recorded, on a large sheet of paper in columns, whether their preference was to be a stonecutter or a prince. They then formed into smaller groups to discuss the advantages and disadvantages of each lifestyle. At the end of the session they recast their votes. The outcome was a strong swing away from the attraction of being a prince. Most children had moved towards a position of thoughtful uncertainty.

On another occasion a discussion about whether or not aliens existed or not led to a surprising outcome. Initially children focused on the threat from intelligent alien life. But after a while, and having recorded feelings about the idea of being alone in the universe, it became clear that there could be unexpected advantages in an alien landing. Again what emerged were the shades of grey, rather than the very clear-cut positions that were expressed at the outset.

The opportunity to agree or disagree and to consider a choice of theories seems to encourage a noticing of thinking processes and produces rich metaphors of the mind. This is how Justin, aged ten, expresses it

> Philosophy helps me . . . well, juggling things in my mind really to think about what I am thinking. Like if there is a question like, 'Do you believe in aliens, don't you believe in aliens?' . . . You might think you don't believe in them and then a question comes up that tells you more about it, so you change.

Other features that children have commented on include the sense of freedom to explore different questions and the calm and relaxed atmosphere that makes it easier to listen. They speak of the pleasure of thinking their own thoughts. Some refer to a sense of greater self-control.

## The views of teachers in one village school

In a school where children have practised philosophical enquiry over a few years teachers report a variety of changes that they have observed in their pupils. The teacher of the class of four to seven-year-olds noticed a greater diversity of ideas in discussion as well as children's increased ability to build on each other's ideas.

Whenever the children listened to a story they asked many more questions and they showed greater interest in the motives of characters in stories. When looking at books by themselves the teacher noticed more evidence of interaction with pictures and with text. She also noticed that the children were using the language introduced in enquiry sessions at other times in class. Children were fascinated in particular with a discussion that had arisen on how to be still both 'outside and inside'.

The teacher responsible for the class of junior pupils, aged seven to eleven, was particularly aware of changes in children's levels of social skills. She reported increased levels of co-operation between all pupils in the class, more effective collaboration in group work and enhanced ability to negotiate with one another. Pupils appeared more confident and more ready and able to articulate their ideas and express their feelings and opinions.

The gains claimed by children and teachers above seem to endorse the view expressed by Carol McGuiness (1999: 2). She suggests:

> developing better thinking and reasoning skills may have much to do with creating dispositions for good thinking as it has to do with acquiring specific skills and strategies. For this reason classrooms need to have open-minded attitudes about the nature of knowledge and to create an educational atmosphere where talking about thinking – questioning, predicting, contradicting, doubting – is not only tolerated but actively pursued.

## Improvements in the use of English

In the UK (as well as in other English-speaking countries) there is evidence to suggest that regular practice of philosophical enquiry leads to significant gains in children's overall use of English. Teachers will immediately recognise the importance for the wider curriculum of a good command of the language used for learning.

Improved attainment in speaking and listening is an area recognised in inspection reports of schools where the practice has been adopted throughout the school (Ofsted, 1997, 1998). Ofsted's report on Wapping First School (1997) concludes:

> In speaking and listening standards of attainment are good and pupils make good progress. Many pupils enter the nursery with low levels of attainment in speaking. By the end of Key Stage 1 pupils speak with confidence, are able to respond to questions and to listen to each other in discussions. By the end of Key Stage 2, pupils can use an appropriate vocabulary to engage the listener and take an active part in discussions when opportunities are presented. An example of this was in the philosophy lesson when pupils demonstrated their ability to discuss ideas, listen with concentration and question each other's ideas and opinions.

In a research study carried out in schools in one Welsh local education authority on the use of thinking skills programmes, the impact on listening and discussion skills was also identified:

Observations carried out by the project team recorded that most of the 5–6 year old children became better listeners as the project progressed, sustaining concentration and an interest in the views of others for up to an hour.

(Dyfed LEA, 1994)

## Reading, reasoning and learning

The study by Dyfed Local Education Authority showed benefits for pupils' reading, thinking and self-esteem. The study was carried out with Year 1 pupils and involved eighteen primary schools. The Improving Reading Standards in Primary Schools Project (Dyfed LEA, 1994) evaluated two teaching approaches: a thinking skills programme based on the work of Karin Murris (1992) and a 'reading activity' designed to enhance the transfer of thinking skills to reading.

In terms of reading, pupils who had done philosophy made more gains in reading than those who had not, although the gains did not reach a statistically significant level. (Given the age of the pupils and the length of the project, this is not surprising.) Many pupils reported that they were more able to think of ideas, and that this activity helped them with their reading and writing. Teachers attributed a greater interest in books and improved reading skills to the thinking skills approach.

In terms of thinking and reasoning the children had more ideas as a result of the intervention, not only in philosophy sessions but also in other areas of the curriculum. One teacher reported feedback from parents indicating that their children were thinking and questioning more at home. Confronted with a problem situation they were better 'able to grasp more than the immediate consequences of the problem and could see issues relating to more than one side of the problem' (Dyfed LEA, 1994).

## Inclusion of all pupils

This study is not alone in identifying as one of the most important gains an increase in pupils' self-esteem as a result of being involved in discussion where their ideas are given credence. The report states:

> The children's enthusiasm for the process, their increasing partic-
> ipation and the increase in quality and quantity of ideas were all
> evidence of the children's growth in their belief in themselves as
> thinkers. The children's growth in self-esteem was most obvious
> in those who at the outset were either withdrawn or unfocused in

their participation, but who by the end were joining in with confidence and making relevant contributions respectively.

(Dyfed LEA, 1994)

The Dyfed LEA report on this project also provides five brief case studies of children with special educational needs who in particular benefited from the thinking skills work based on the approach developed by Murris (1992), using picture books as a starting point for enquiry. The 'flourishing' of this group of children is often reported by teachers adopting the approach, in the sense that children change from sometimes tearful, restless or very passive and withdrawn ('invisible') to becoming more cheerful, outgoing, active participants being able to concentrate better on the task in hand.

These findings concur with the comments made by Carol McGuiness (1999) on the benefits of philosophy with children. In her summary of the different thinking skills approaches (p. 3) she writes:

> The approach can be used across the curriculum particularly in the context of social and moral education where the philosophical emphasis is on questioning and questioning is important. Evaluations show positive effects along many dimensions other than standardised achievement tests, for example, in terms of the quality of children's discussion and argumentative skills, ability to formulate questions, self-esteem, and so on.

## Thinking schools

The most obvious areas of the curriculum to benefit from open-ended dialogue are English, the Humanities, and Personal and Social Education. But inspection and research reports refer to school ethos, to pupils' social and moral development and to increased independence of thought and to using a range of learning skills and strategies. In making sense of such findings we need to bear in mind that, on the whole, those schools that are considering the inclusion of regular philosophical discussion in their timetables are also exploring other thinking and enquiry-based approaches to learning across the curriculum.

A number of schools in East Anglia are now embarked on a project called Thinking Schools – Thinking Children with funding from the local education authority in Norfolk. Teachers in these schools are engaged in action research to identify and disseminate successful practice. Schools in Cornwall have established a network to share ideas in promoting children's thinking and learning. These developments open up promising possibilities for teachers and learners alike.

# Appendix 1
## Useful addresses and contacts

*Society for the Advancement of Philosophical Enquiry and Reflection in Education (SAPERE)*
For information or queries: Sara Liptai, 7 Cloister Way, Leamington Spa CV32 6QE England
E-mail sara.liptai@altergo.co.uk
www.sapere.net

*Dialogueworks: for resources and training in philosophy with children*
www.dialogueworks.co.uk
E-mail enquiries@dialogueworks.co.uk

*International Council for Philosophical Inquiry with Children (ICPIC)*
Secretary: Cecilia Hornell (Sweden)
E-mail cecilia.hornell@sodrateatern.com

*Institute for the Advancement of Philosophy for Children (IAPC)*
Director: Dr Ann Margaret Sharp, Montclair State University, Upper Montclair NJ 07043, USA
E-mail sharp@saturn.montclair.edu.

# Appendix 2

## Resources for philosophy with children

### Books and materials for the classroom

Fisher. R. (1996) *Stories for Thinking*. Oxford: Nash Pollock.
Fisher R. (1997) *Games for Thinking*. Oxford: Nash Pollock.
Fisher R. (1997) *Poems for Thinking*. Oxford: Nash Pollock.
Fox R. (1996) *Thinking Matters: Stories to Encourage Thinking Skills*.
  Exeter: Southgate Publishers.
Murris, K. and Haynes, J. *Storywise: Thinking through Stories*.
  Available from www.dialogueworks.co.uk
Williams, S. and Sutcliffe, R. *Newswise: Thinking through the News*.
  Available from www.dialogueworks.co.uk

Videos of many picture books are available from Channel 4 Schools,
PO Box 100, Warwick CV34 6TZ. Tel. (01926) 436444.
www.channel4.com/schools/shop

### Journals

*Journal 100* (written by children)
Edited by Berrie Heesen, Netherlands
www.xs4all.nl/~krant100/engels/eindex.html

*Teaching Thinking*. Questions Publishing, 27 Frederick Street,
Birmingham B1 3HH. www.teachthinking.com

*Thinking: the Journal of Philosophy for Children*, edited by David
Kennedy
www.bgsu.edu/offices/phildoc/thinking.html

*Analytic Teaching*, edited by Richard Morehouse
www.viterbo.edu/campnews/camppub/analytic/index.htm

*Critical and Creative Thinking: the Australasian Journal of Philosophy for Children*, edited by Clive Lindop
E-mail clivel@deakin.edu.au

## General reference for teachers

Cam, P. (1995) *Thinking Together: Philosophical Inquiry for the Classroom*. Sydney: Hale and Ironmonger.

De Botton, A. (2000) *The Consolations of Philosophy*. London: Hamish Hamilton.

Fisher, R. (1999) *Teaching Thinking: Philosophical Enquiry in the Classroom*. London: Cassell.

Law, S. (2000) *The Philosophy Files*. London: Orion.

Lipman, M. (ed.) (1993) *Thinking, Children and Education*. Dubuque IA: Kendall/Hunt.

Magee, B. (1998) *The Story of Philosophy*. London: Dorling Kindersley.

Warburton, N. (1995) *Philosophy: The Basics*. Second edition, London: Routledge.

# References

Abbs, P. (1994) *The Educational Imperative: A Defence of Socratic and Aesthetic Learning*. London: Falmer Press.

Adey, P. and Shayer, M. (1994) *Really Raising Standards: Cognitive Intervention and Academic Achievement*. London: Routledge.

Advisory Group on Citizenship chaired by Professor Bernard Crick (1998) *Education for Citizenship and the Teaching of Democracy in Schools*. London: DfEE and QCA.

Bachelard, G. (1971) *The Poetics of Reverie: Childhood, Language and the Cosmos*. Boston MA: Beacon Press.

Ball, S. (1994) Address to the Annual Standing Conference for Studies in Education held at the RSA, London.

Blagg, N., Ballinger, M. and Gardner, R. (1988) *Somerset Thinking Skills Course*. Oxford: Basil Blackwell.

Bonnett, M. (1994) *Children's Thinking: Promoting Understanding in the Primary School*. London: Cassell.

Bonnett, M. (1995) 'Teaching Thinking and the Sanctity of Content', *Journal of Philosophy of Education* 29 (3): 295–309.

Boyle, J. (2001) 'You can count me out', *Observer Review*, 14 January.

Bradman, T. (1990) *Michael*. Illustrated by Tony Ross. London: Andersen Press.

Bruner, J. (1996) *The Culture of Education*. Boston, MA: Harvard University Press.

Cam, P. (1995) *Thinking Together: Philosophical Inquiry for the Classroom*. Sydney: Primary English Teaching Association and Hale and Iremonger.

Clark, A. and Moss, P. (2001) *Listening to Young Children: The Mosaic Approach*. London: Routledge.

Claxton, G. (1997) *Hare Brain, Tortoise Mind*. London: Fourth Estate.

Claxton, G. (1999) *Wise Up*. London: Bloomsbury.

Cleary, T. (1993) *Lao Tze in the essential Tao*. San Francisco: Harper.

Corradi Fiumara, G. (1992) *The Other Side of Language: A Philosophy of Listening*. London: Routledge.

Corradi Fiumara, G. (1995) *The Metaphoric Process: Connections between Language and Life*. London: Routledge.

De Botton, A. (2000) *The Consolations of Philosophy*. London: Hamish Hamilton.

Department for Education and Employment and Qualifications and Curriculum Authority (1999) *The National Curriculum Handbook for Primary Teachers in England: Key Stages 1 and 2*. London: DfEE and QCA

Department for Education and Employment and Qualifications and Curriculum Authority (2000) *The Foundation Stage Curriculum*. London: DfEE and QCA

Dewey, J. (1963) *Experience and Education*. New York: Collier Macmillan.

Dewey, J. (1966) *Democracy and Education: an Introduction to the Philosophy of Education*. New York: Free Press.

Donaldson, M. (1978) *Children's Minds*. London: Fontana.

Donaldson, M. (1992) *Human Minds: An Exploration*. London: Penguin.

Dyfed Local Education Authority (1994) *The Improving Reading Standards in Primary Schools Project Report*. Carmarthen: Dyfed LEA

Edwards, C., Gandini, L., and Forman, G. (1998) *The Hundred Languages of Children: The Reggio Emilia Approach Advanced Reflections*. London: Ablex.

Egan, K. (1988) *Teaching as Storytelling: an Alternative Approach to Teaching and the Curriculum*. London ONT: University of Western Ontario.

Egan, K. (1991) *Primary Understanding: Education in Early Childhood*. London: Routledge.

Feyerabend, P. (1994) *Killing Time*. Chicago: University of Chicago Press.

Fisher, R. (1990) *Teaching Children to Think*. Hemel Hempstead: Simon & Schuster.

Fisher, R. (1995) *Teaching Children to Learn*. London: Stanley Thornes.

Fisher, R. (1996) *Stories for Thinking*. Oxford: Nash Pollock.

Fisher, R. (1997) *Games for Thinking*. Oxford: Nash Pollock.

Fisher, R. (1998) *Teaching Thinking: Philosophical Enquiry in the Classroom*. London: Cassell.

Fontana, D. and Slack, I. (1997) *Teaching Meditation to Children*. Shaftesbury: Element.

Gaarder, J. (1997) *Hello! Is Anybody There?* Illustrated by Sally Gardner. London: Orion.

Gardner, H. (1999) *Intelligence Reframed. Multiple Intelligences for the Twenty-first Century*. New York: Basic Books.

Gardner, S. (1996) 'Inquiry is no mere Conversation', *Analytic Teaching* 16 (2): 41–7.

Glover, J. (1999) Interview in *The Guardian*, 13 October.

Glover, J. (2001) *Humanity: a Moral History of the Twentieth Century*. London: Pimlico.

Habermas, J. (1990) *Moral Consciousness and Communicative Action*. Cambridge: Polity Press.

Haynes, J. (2000) 'Take a deep breath', *Teaching Thinking* 2: 26–8.

Haynes, J. and Murris, K. (2000) 'Listening, juggling and travelling in philosophical space', *Critical and Creative Thinking: Australasian Journal of Philosophy for Children* 8 (1): 23–32.

Heidegger, M. (1966) *Discourse on Thinking*. New York: Harper and Row.

Heidegger, M. and Krell, D. F. (eds) (1993) *Martin Heidegger: Basic Writings*. London: Routledge.

Heine, H. (1983) *The Most Wonderful Egg in the World*. New York: Macmillan, Aladdin Books.

Holden, C. and Clough, N. (eds) (1998) *Children as Citizens: Education for Participation*. London: Jessica Kingsley.

Hughes, J. (1995) 'The philosopher's child', *Thinking: Journal of Philosophy for Children* 10 (1): 38–44.

Hutchins, P. (1987) *Changes, Changes*. New York: Macmillan, Aladdin Books.

Jackson, A. (1999) *The Book of Life*. London: Gollancz.

Keats, E. J. (1977) *Whistle with Willie*. Harmondsworth: Puffin Books.

Kellogg, S. (1973) *The Island of the Skog*. New York: Penguin, Pied Piper.

Kelly, A. V. (1995) *Education and Democracy: Principles and Practices*. London: Paul Chapman.

Kennedy, D. (1992) 'Why Philosophy for Children Now?' *Thinking: Journal of Philosophy for Children* 10 (3): 2–6.

Kennedy, D. (1999) 'Philosophy for Children and the Reconstruction of Philosophy'. Paper submitted to the Conference of the Society of Consultant Philosophers, Wadham College, Oxford.

Lakoff, G. and Johnson, M. (1980) *Metaphors we Live by*. Chicago: University of Chicago Press.

Lakoff, G. and Johnson, M. (1999) *Philosophy in the Flesh: The Embodied Mind and its Challenge to Western Thought*. London: Harper Collins.

Lao Tzu (1963) *Tao te ching*, trans. D. C. Lau. London: Penguin.

Law, S. (2000) *The Philosophy Files*. London: Orion.

Levin, D. M. (1989) *The Listening Self: Personal Growth, Social Change and the Closure of Metaphysics*. London: Routledge.

Lipman, M. (1981) *Pixie*. Montclair NJ: New Jersey Institute for the Advancement of Philosophy for Children.

Lipman, M. (1985) *Lisa*. Montclair NJ: New Jersey Institute for the Advancement of Philosophy for Children.

Lipman, M. (1991) *Thinking in Education*. Cambridge: Cambridge University Press.

Lipman, M. (ed.) (1993) *Thinking, Children and Education*. Dubuque IA: Kendall/Hunt.

Lipman, M. (1997) 'Philosophical Discussion: Plans and Exercises', *Critical and Creative Thinking* 5 (1): 1–17.

McDermott, G. (1975) *The Stonecutter*. Harmondsworth: Puffin.

McEwan, I. (1994) *The Daydreamer*. Illustrated by Anthony Browne. London: Random House Red Fox.

McGuiness, C. (1999) *From Thinking Skills to Thinking Classrooms*. DfEE Research Report 115. London: Department for Education and Employment.

McKee, D. (1980) *Not Now, Bernard*. London: Random House Red Fox.

McKee, D. (1991) 'The Sad Story of Veronica who Played the Violin' on video: *Not Now, Bernard and other Stories by David McKee*. London: Abbey Broadcast Communications.

Magee, B. (1998) *The Story of Philosophy*. London: Dorling Kindersley.

Mason, J. H. (1996) *Personal Enquiry: Moving from Concern towards Research*. Mathematics Education Monograph R: MA in Education, ME822. Buckingham: Open University Press.

Matthews, G. B. (1980) *Philosophy and the Young Child*. Boston MA: Harvard University Press.

Matthews, G. B. (1984) *Dialogues with Children*. Boston MA: Harvard University Press.

Meek, J. (1999) 'Into the garden of good and evil' in The Guardian 13 October, 1999.

Midgley, M. (1995) *Wisdom, Information and Wonder: What is Knowledge for?* London: Routledge.

Mills, C. and Mills, D. (1998) *Dispatches: The Early Years*. London: Channel 4 Television.

Mortimore, P. (ed.) (1999) *Understanding Pedagogy and its Impact on Learning*. London: Paul Chapman.

Mosley, J. (2000) *Quality Circle Time in Action* (video and booklet). Wisbech: LDA.

Murris, K. (1992) *Teaching Philosophy with Picture Books*. London: Infonet.

Murris, K. (1997) 'Metaphors of the Child's Mind: Teaching Philosophy to Young Children' Ph.D. thesis, University of Hull.

Murris, K. and Haynes, J. (2000) Storywise. www.dialogueworks.co.uk

Ofsted (1997) *Inspection Report: Wapping First School*. Norwich: Ofsted.

Ofsted (1998) *Inspection Report: Tuckswood First School*. Norwich: Ofsted.

Pinney, R. (1983) *Creative Listening*. London: A to Z Printers & Publishers.

Quinn, V. (1997) *Critical Thinking in Young Minds*. London: David Fulton.

Rosenow, E. (1993) 'Plato, Dewey and the Problem of the Teacher's Authority', *Journal of Philosophy of Education* 27 (2): 209–21.

Sendak, M. (1992) *Where the Wild Things Are*. London: Harper Collins Picture Lions.

Splitter, L. and Sharp, A. M. (1995) *Teaching for Better Thinking*. Melbourne: Australian Council for Educational Research.

Stevens, A. (1999) 'The Millennium Phenomenon and Apocalyptic Thinking' lecture at the annual Ways with Words festival, Dartington Hall.

Tripp, D. (1993) *Critical Incidents in Teaching: Developing Professional Judgment*. London: Routledge.

Ungerer, T. (1961) *The Three Robbers*. London: Methuen.

UNICEF (1995) *The Convention on the Rights of the Child*. London: UK Committee for UNICEF.

Wagner, J. (1977) *John Brown, Rose and the Midnight Cat*. Illustrated by Ron Brooks. Harmondsworth: Viking Kestrel.

Weikart, D., Rogers, L., Adcock, C. and McLelland, D. (1971) *The Cognitively Orientated Curriculum: A Framework for Pre-school Teachers*, Urbana IL: University of Illinois Press.

Winnicott, D. (1971) *Playing and Reality*. London: Tavistock Publications.

Woods, P. (1995) *Creative Teachers in Primary Schools*. Buckingham: Open University Press.

Woods, P. and Jeffrey, B. (1996) *Teachable Moments: The Art of Teaching in Primary Schools*. Buckingham: Open University Press.

Zeldin, T. (1998) *Conversation*. London: Harvill Press.

# Index